D0200945

THE HARD
COUNT

THE HARD COUNT

The Political and Social Challenges of Census Mobilization

D. Sunshine Hillygus,
Norman H. Nie,
Kenneth Prewitt, and
Heili Pals

Russell Sage Foundation
New York

The Russell Sage Foundation

The Russell Sage Foundation, one of the oldest of America's general purpose foundations, was established in 1907 by Mrs. Margaret Olivia Sage for "the improvement of social and living conditions in the United States." The Foundation seeks to fulfill this mandate by fostering the development and dissemination of knowledge about the country's political, social, and economic problems. While the Foundation endeavors to assure the accuracy and objectivity of each book it publishes, the conclusions and interpretations in Russell Sage Foundation publications are those of the authors and not of the Foundation, its Trustees, or its staff. Publication by Russell Sage, therefore, does not imply Foundation endorsement.

BOARD OF TRUSTEES
Thomas D. Cook, Chair

Alan S. Blinder	John A. Ferejohn	Alan B. Krueger
Kenneth D. Brody	Larry V. Hedges	Cora B. Marrett
Christine K. Cassel	Jennifer L. Hochschild	Eric Wanner
Robert E. Denham	Kathleen Hall Jamieson	Mary C. Waters
Christopher Edley Jr.	Melvin J. Konner	

Library of Congress Cataloging-in-Publication Data

The Hard Count : the political and social challenges of census mobilization / D. Sunshine Hillygus . . . [et al.].
    p. cm.
    ISBN 0-87154-363-X
    1. United States—Census—History. 2. United States—Population—History. 3. United States—Census, 2000. I. Hillygus, D. Sunshine.

HA181.C68 2006
317.3—dc22

2005057522

Copyright © 2006 by Russell Sage Foundation. All rights reserved. Printed in the United States of America. No part of this publication may be reproduced, stored in a retrieval system, or transmitted in any form or by any means, electronic, mechanical, photocopying, recording, or otherwise, without the prior written permission of the publisher.

Reproduction by the United States Government in whole or in part is permitted for any purpose.

The paper used in this publication meets the minimum requirements of American National Standard for Information Sciences—Permanence of Paper for Printed Library Materials. ANSI Z39.48-1992.

Text design by Genna Patacsil.

RUSSELL SAGE FOUNDATION
112 East 64th Street, New York, New York 10021
10 9 8 7 6 5 4 3 2 1

To the memory of Daniel Patrick Moynihan

A social scientist who understood policymaking and a
policymaker who understood the contribution
of the social sciences. On the topic at hand,
he wisely observed: "There is simply nothing so important to a people as how many of them there are,
whether the number is growing or declining, how they
are distributed between ages, sexes and different social
classes and racial and ethnic groups, and … which
way these numbers are moving" (Moynihan 1977, 89).

Contents |

About the Authors |

D. SUNSHINE HILLYGUS is assistant professor of government at Harvard University.

NORMAN H. NIE is director of the Stanford Institute for the Quantitative Study of Society at Stanford University.

KENNETH PREWITT is Carnegie Professor of Public Affairs in the School of International and Public Affairs at Columbia University.

HEILI PALS is a doctoral candidate in sociology at Stanford University.

Acknowledgments |

THIS RESEARCH WOULD not have been possible without the generous support of The Russell Sage Foundation and a consortium of private foundations including The Ford Foundation, The William and Flora Hewlett Foundation, The Annie E. Casey Foundation, The John D. and Catherine T. MacArthur Foundation, The Andrew W. Mellon Foundation, and The Carnegie Corporation of New York. Sunshine Hillygus also received financial support from the Institute for Quantitative Social Sciences at Harvard University. The Russell Sage Foundation provided further support for this project with a visiting scholar position for Ken Prewitt while this book was in preparation.

We would like to thank multiple cohorts of research assistants at the Stanford Institute for the Quantitative Study of Society for their hard work and effort on this project, especially Markus Prior, Sunny Niu, Jennifer Lawless, Shawn Treier and Hahrie Han. We are also deeply indebted to Emily Borom, SIQSS senior administrator, for her efforts and assistance.

Our many thanks to the publications staff of the Russell Sage Foundation, who have helped make for an exceptionally smooth publication process. We are especially grateful to Suzanne Nichols for her continuous patience, enthusiasm, and support. The final manuscript was much improved by the red pen of copyeditor, Cindy Buck, and the constructive comments of the anonymous reviewers.

Finally, a special acknowledgment goes to Jane Junn for her many contributions to this project.

Introduction |

The actual enumeration shall be made within three
years after the first meeting of the Congress of the
United States, and within every subsequent term of ten
years, in such manner as they shall by law direct.

—*Constitution of the United States of America*, article I, section 2

THE DECENNIAL CENSUS sounds so simple. Just count everyone across the
nation and add up the numbers. Yet this seemingly mundane task is anything but simple and more than a little controversial. The census contro-
versies in 2000, for instance, focused on issues of representation for
minorities, privacy and confidentiality, and partisan politics. The political
stakes of census participation are high. The decennial population count
determines the number of seats a state gets in Congress and forms the basis
for redrawing congressional districts and other political boundaries within
a state. The census figures are used to distribute billions of dollars each year
in federal grants to states and localities for everything from education to
highways. Given that two of the most fundamental government com-
modities—money and representation—are linked to the census count, it is
hardly surprising that it fuels political battles.

At the center of census politics is the fact that no population count is
completely accurate. Moreover, some individuals in society are more difficult to count than others, and these undercounted individuals are disproportionately ethnic and racial minorities. Every decision regarding the
undercount is fraught with practical and political considerations. Deciding
which procedures to implement to ensure the most complete count, how
to estimate the undercount, whether to use adjusted population figures—
these are all difficult decisions with political consequences. Because of those
consequences, congressional involvement in and oversight of the 2000 census was unprecedented. Starting two years before the census, the director
of the Census Bureau, Kenneth Prewitt, testified before Congress 23 times,
responded to over 150 letters from the House Subcommittee on the Census

(which itself held 17 hearings on Census 2000 design issues), and cooperated with 522 field visits by the U.S. General Accounting Office, the Congressional Monitoring Board, and the Commerce Department inspector general. Members of Congress as well as half a dozen executive branch advisory committees had strong views about how the census should be conducted. Before arriving in Washington to begin his term, Prewitt was repeatedly told that he was accepting an impossible task. After a few weeks in the job, he quipped that the task must not be so difficult after all because he had yet to meet anyone not prepared to tell him how to do it.

In the prosperous economy of the 1990s, there was agreement across the political aisle on one major issue: the Census Bureau should attempt to improve the traditional population count by mounting a massive (and expensive) promotional campaign aimed at mobilizing public cooperation. It is a difficult task to motivate a diverse, mobile, and sometimes distrustful society to participate in a civic activity for which there is little obvious individual benefit. But toward that goal, the bureau designed an effort that would become characterized as the "largest peacetime mobilization" in U.S. history.

Our initial research aim was to monitor this mobilization effort in real time, rigorously evaluating the effectiveness of the census campaign. Originally the project was broadly motivated by two key motivating questions: What explains why some people participate in the census and others do not? And is there something the Census Bureau can do to stimulate participation? In the midst of the campaign, however, issues of privacy and confidentiality unexpectedly emerged as a focus of census controversy. Given the bipartisan support for the mobilization effort, the Census Bureau was unprepared for a political debate that would ultimately question the bureau's very right to collect census data beyond a basic head count. This debate centered on the census long form: within the heightened political context of an election year, and with growing public concern about privacy issues, an acrimonious controversy emerged regarding the form's intrusiveness. Some of the same political leaders who had approved each of the questions on the long-form questionnaire now encouraged individuals not to fully complete the census. Congressman Ron Paul, for instance, introduced legislation to prohibit the Census Bureau from collecting any information from citizens except name, address, and the number of people per residence, on the justification that "all of this additional information being requested by the Census Bureau is a major intrusion on the privacy of American citizens."[1] Although this and similar bills failed, criticism of the census was widespread. The concern focused primarily on a few long-form questions but expanded into a larger discussion about the privacy and confidentiality of the census generally. Thus, this book has also come to focus on the influence of the privacy debate on public attitudes and census cooperation. More specifically we ask whether the privacy controversy that arose during the mobilization campaign depressed census participation among some segments of the population. And we assess the extent to which the negative rhetoric about the census long form may have influenced cooperation with the census short form as well.

Just one year before the census, the majority of Americans were unaware that a census count would even take place (Belden Russonello and Stewart Research and Communications 1999). The publicity campaign was launched in late 1999 and gathered enough momentum leading up to Census Day—April 1, 2000—that it was successful in building public awareness of the census; by March 2000, with the mobilization campaign in full swing, the privacy debate had found an audience primed to hear census-related messages, even messages, it turned out, that pulled in opposite directions. From one side, there were positive, reassuring statements about the census from civic leaders, local politicians, and a massive advertising campaign that collectively emphasized the civic benefits of census cooperation. At the same time, though for a much briefer period, the public was bombarded with negative rhetoric, especially from talk show hosts and editorial pages, but also from highly visible political personalities. Here the repeated message was that the census was an unwarranted invasion of privacy. Thus, the experience of the 2000 census provides a real-world opportunity to explore a classic social science question about the role and influence of competing information campaigns and, on a more fundamental level, to look at the determinants of civic participation.

Our analysis of the effects of the mobilization campaign and the privacy debate has two broad purposes. First, we hope that our analysis of census participation from a social science perspective will contribute to a theoretical understanding of the impact of competing information campaigns on the attitudes and behavior of the American public. Second, our evaluation of the 2000 census experience will be helpful to the Census Bureau as it prepares for the decennial census in 2010 and beyond. Here we apply the findings from our theoretically motivated empirical analysis to the practicalities of policymaking to help answer the fundamental question of why some households willingly return their census forms and others do not.

Thus, this book was written with both social science scholars and census policymakers in mind. We recognize the difficulty of trying to speak to a diverse readership. Some readers may view our coverage of social science research and theories to be incomplete, while others may consider that discussion irrelevant. Some readers may view our empirical analysis as too focused on methodological technicalities, while others may view it as not technical enough. But these are risks worth taking. Far too often academics and policymakers do not share their learned knowledge, and as a result research and social commentary only rarely converge. We believe that policy advice should be rooted in neutral social science analysis, and that social scientists should account for real-world politics in their analysis and consider the practical implications of their findings. In this book, we attempt to translate social science findings into policy recommendations, applying the results of our empirical analysis to the known constraints and likely developments in census-taking. As such, we hope this book contributes to both improved census enumerations and broader social science research about civic participation in American society.

WHY STUDY THE CENSUS?

For those of us who study political and social behavior, statistical data about the U.S. population are our livelihood. All branches of empirical social science—research on labor market behavior, social mobility, educational attainment, urbanization, the dynamics of race relations, immigrant assimilation, and on and on—use data from the nation's statistical agencies, which are based on one level or another on the decennial census. Of course, government survey and statistical data are not generated, at a cost of approximately $5 billion a year (excluding decennial census costs), to satisfy the empirical social sciences. Public policy, democratic accountability, social justice, and commercial activities—to name only the most obvious applications—draw on statistics about the size, geographic distribution, and other relevant characteristics of America's population and establishments. These statistics, collected by seventy federal agencies, come directly from individuals and organizations that complete forms. The decennial census is the heart and backbone of our national statistical system, the largest source of statistical data, and the benchmark against which other surveys are calibrated. It is therefore critical to understand why some individuals cooperate with the census count while others do not.

Like most social scientists, one of the authors of this book had casually assumed the strength of the nation's statistical system, but experiencing that system at its core—directing the Census Bureau during a decennial census—was sobering. The robustness of this system rests on a fragile base—the willingness of the American public to check boxes and fill in blanks. If this willingness falters, as it may, either there will be no national statistical system or, much more likely, the government and the commercial sector will devise an information system based on administrative records and involuntary surveillance, data sources that do not, at least presently, have the same level of quality control that is built into the census and sample-based surveys. The stakes are not trivial.

Throughout our analysis, we define census cooperation as voluntarily mailing back the census form. Since 1970, the Census Bureau has mailed a census form to every known American household with a postal address, to be completed and mailed back. (Five-sixths of households receive the short form, and the remaining one-sixth receive the long form, which also includes all short-form questions.) The Census Bureau must send employees door to door to enumerate the households that do not return a form, at considerable cost and effort. Although the households counted by census enumerators do technically cooperate in the population count, participation by mail-back form is more cost-effective and produces higher-quality data. Thus, our interest is in understanding the many factors—both internal and external to a household—that shape mail-back cooperation.

Although census cooperation is required by law, mailing back the form is ultimately voluntary, since households can fulfill their legal duty by waiting until an enumerator knocks on the door. The Census Bureau acknowledged during the 2000 count that it did not intend to bring legal action against anyone who avoided the census or even outright refused to cooperate. The bureau's reasoning was simple—initiating legal action could backfire and reduce more than increase cooperation. Moreover, a national census simply would not be logistically possible without voluntary cooperation (Bulmer 1979; Melnick 1981). Thus, there remains considerable variation in census cooperation to be explained, not only in mail-back participation but in the completeness of the forms returned. Thus, even though the census is mandated by law, there is much to be learned about why some participate in this civic activity and others do not.

CENSUS PARTICIPATION

As we look at the predictors of census participation, it is helpful to emphasize that, like other forms of civic or political participation, census cooperation requires both the capacity and the motivation to participate (Verba, Schlozman, and Brady 1995). The census mobilization campaign was focused on motivating all American households to participate, but throughout our analysis we also take into account that some households are better equipped than others with the skills and resources necessary for census cooperation. Although the skills required for completing a census short form may be lower than the skills needed for other forms of civic and political participation, census cooperation nonetheless requires some basic skills and resources. The complex and difficult-to-understand residency rules, for example, are necessary to capture the great variety in household composition across the country. Completing and returning a census form (either short or long form) is no doubt more difficult for the illiterate, the disabled, and the non-English-speaking.[2] And for the census long form, more extensive skills—such as an ability to follow complicated instructions, math skills to calculate requested estimates, and reading comprehension skills—may be needed to fully and accurately answer the questions. In addition to these basic skills, census form completion requires time. Although the minutes it takes to complete a census form every ten years may seem like a rather minor obligation, a decade horizon is not the context in which most people judge the burden. Rather, the minutes required to fill out a census form come directly from the time an individual has today—or even the shorter amount of time available after the workday has ended, the kids have been fed, and the daily chores are done. Within that context, the census long form might be viewed as a particularly steep burden. And even the few minutes required to complete the short form inevitably come at the expense of some other activity. To an increasingly hurried and harried public, answering the census questions is more likely to be viewed as a nuisance than an opportunity.

Beyond time and skills, census participation requires motivation. Individuals must ultimately make a conscious and deliberate choice to undertake the action of completing the census form. The particular motivation behind cooperating with the census may vary for different individuals. Some may be motivated by a sense of civic duty. Others may be motivated by a material desire to bring more resources to their community. Still others may be motivated by social pressures from friends, family, or neighbors (or children—there was a significant push within the public schools to increase the cooperation of households with school-age children). And there are some who are no doubt grudgingly motivated by the simple fact that census cooperation is mandatory, reasoning that it is easier to fill out the form than to have an enumerator come knocking on the door at a later date. The challenge for the Census Bureau, then, was to create a mobilization campaign that could somehow motivate a busy public to cooperate with the census count.

BACKGROUND AND CONTRIBUTION

In examining census cooperation in the context of the mobilization effort and the privacy debate, we address both theoretical and empirical questions about civic participation and the influence of information campaigns on mass attitudes and behavior. As such, our analysis is grounded in and builds on theories from political science, political psychology, and mass communication. To this broad literature our analysis offers three primary contributions. First, we extend the extensive research on campaign effects (both political and information-based) with a rigorous evaluation of the massive census mobilization campaign, using a unique methodological design and investigating possible differential effects within the population. Second, we take advantage of the quasi-natural experiment created with the eruption of the privacy debate to examine the effect of competing census messages, thus building on the framing effects literature. Finally, with our examination of the empirical links between census participation and other forms of civic and political engagement, our study has implications for the classic research on civic engagement and social capital. We offer a brief background on each of these bodies of research in turn.

Studies focused on the influence of information campaigns on public attitudes date to the early 1900s. Prewar theories of what in that period was labeled propaganda assumed that the public could easily be swayed by media messages (Lasswell 1927; Lippmann 1922). Indeed, many scholars feared that the media had the power to shape and control the ideas, attitudes, and behaviors of the mass public. Yet the earliest empirical studies found that political campaigns and media messages had only a minimal impact on public attitudes (Berelson, Lazarsfeld, and McPhee 1954; Klapper 1960; Lazarsfeld, Berelson, and Gauzet 1948). This minimal effects perspective became the conventional wisdom for the next half-century, with scholars concluding that "mass communications ordinarily do not serve as a necessary and sufficient cause of audience [persuasion] effects . . . [and] when mass communication does affect people, these effects tend to be minor and short-lived" (Klapper 1960, 8). In political science, scholars found that they could instead predict civic engagement, political participation, and voter turnout quite adequately by accounting only for fixed socio-economic and political factors. Because civic engagement requires time, skills, and motivation, it is possible to identify who has these necessary resources and who does not. Research has found, for instance, that better-educated, older, wealthier, and more politically interested individuals are significantly more likely to vote, volunteer, and participate (see, for example, Nie, Junn, and Stehlik-Berry 1996; Wolfinger and Rosenstone 1980). Only recently has research found that both individual characteristics and campaign factors—when appropriately measured—are important predictors of civic and political engagement (Hillygus and Jackman 2003; Holbrook 1996; Shaw 1999).

Proponents of various public information campaigns, especially health campaigns, experienced a similar shift in expectations about campaign effects. It was initially assumed that media campaigns could shape the attitudes, beliefs, and behaviors of the mass public, but empirical studies soon found that public health campaigns did not usually engender the anticipated outcomes (Atkin and Wallack 1990; Maccoby and Solomon 1981; Robertson 1976;). Anti-drunk-driving campaigns have been pervasive in recent decades but have been found to have no direct effect on youth binge-drinking or drunk-driving behavior (Yanovitzky and Bennett 1999). One extensive seat-belt advertising campaign was found to have saturated the target market, yet those reporting exposure to the message were no more likely to wear their seat belts (Gantz, Fitzmaurice, and Yoo 1990). The intensive, five-year Minnesota Heart Health Program sought to reduce morbidity and mortality from coronary heart disease using mass media, community organizations, and direct education, but an evaluative study found that it had no appreciable impact on health behaviors or risk factor levels (Luepker et al. 1994). Even Surgeon General C. Everett Koop's massive AIDS/HIV information campaign, which included an informational mailing to every U.S. household, could not be directly linked to changes in risky behaviors or increases in knowledge about the virus (Singer, Rogers, and Glassman 1991). As Lawrence Wallack (1990, 370) laments, "The mass media are not the magic bullet of health promotion and disease prevention."

The apparent ineffectiveness of political and health information campaigns contrasts starkly with the obvious success of commercial advertising. Advertising agencies can offer thousands of examples of products flying off the shelves after an extended marketing effort. Civic mobilization is quite different, however. Whereas the purpose of commercial advertising is to persuade an individual that he or she will benefit from a product or service, civic mobilization often requires persuading an individual to participate in an activity that has little direct benefit. If the hamburger or children's toy or latest movie gives immediate gratification, voting or filling out a census form is a different kind of sell. Like other forms of civic engagement, census participation is inherently a collective action problem. Cooperating with the census count contributes to an enormous societal and community good but offers little tangible benefit to the participant. The benefits are distant and indirect, getting no closer than the possibility that your local community will receive marginally more federal monies than might otherwise have been the case. As we discuss in chapter 2, the census campaign was developed to emphasize concrete benefits and worked hard to personalize those so that the household would come to see that census cooperation could lead to improved emergency services or local schools. Even still, scholars now recognize that it is exceedingly difficult for an information campaign to influence public attitudes—whether about voting, health, or the census—and it is harder to influence behavior than attitudes. For example, it is much easier to persuade the American public of the health benefits of regular exercise than to persuade them to actually get off the couch. Here, of course, we are ultimately interested in census behavior.

This study extends the campaign effects literature beyond the electoral and public health arenas to focus on the potential for civic mobilization.

Can an overloaded and disengaged society be mobilized to participate in a decennial population count with a massive promotional campaign? What was the impact of the campaign on census awareness, knowledge, opinions, and, most critically, participation? In evaluating the influence of the census campaign, we also examine differential campaign effects within the population. The Census Bureau was particularly concerned about mobilizing the portion of the population historically undercounted, especially racial and ethnic minorities. There is a perverse finding in communications research that information campaigns often benefit only those individuals who are already well informed, thereby actually widening the gap between the "information-rich" and the "information-poor." In other words, campaigns may increase overall levels of knowledge (or participation), but they may also increase information and participation inequalities. This so-called knowledge gap hypothesis has been found to be prevalent in political campaigns and public health campaigns (Berinsky 2005; Gaziano and Gaziano 1996; Hyman and Sheatsley 1947; Kwak 1999; Star and Hughes 1950; Tichenor, Donohue, and Olien 1970).[3] Thus, even though the Census Bureau was particularly concerned about mobilizing the hardest-to-count populations, the knowledge gap hypothesis implies that one consequence of the census mobilization campaign might be to worsen the differential undercount by improving cooperation only among the easiest-to-count populations (suburban whites). In this study, we evaluate the effects of the census campaign for the population as whole, but also examine differential effects for racial and ethnic minorities.

In thinking about the influence of information campaigns, recent mass communications research now recognizes that media effects are often more nuanced and complex than had once been assumed. The impact of an information campaign on the mass public depends on a number of different factors related to the message, source, and receiver. Some messages—especially those that are intense and presented with a unified voice—are more effective than other messages; some message sources—politicians from your own party compared to those from the opposing party—are viewed as more credible than others; and some receivers or audiences—especially those with less passionate views—are more persuadable than others.

Perhaps most simply, it is important to remember that the public is not a tabula rasa: people have existing attitudes and beliefs that interact with any new information they encounter. As such, information campaigns are generally less effective at telling people what to think than at telling them what to think about. Public discussion can be shaped by drawing attention to some issues and not others (agenda-setting) and by focusing on particular aspects of those issues (framing). By framing an issue to emphasize some values and facts over others, information campaigns can lead individuals to focus on those considerations in constructing their opinion (Nelson, Oxley, and Clawson 1997). Thus, even if a campaign does not directly persuade the public with a specific message or advertisement, it can have a profound indirect effect by shaping how the public perceives and evaluates an issue or topic.

Issue framing is critical to public debate because most public issues—certainly the census—are complex. Research has found, for instance, that the less information an individual has about an issue, or the greater his or her degree of ambivalence about it, the greater the possible impact of new information (Druckman 2001; Zaller 1992). Certainly most Americans spend little time thinking about the census. And to the extent that the American public does hold predispositions of relevance to census cooperation, they might include a wide range of attitudes and values, some of which might be in conflict. For instance, an individual might feel a basic commitment to civic responsibility but also have reservations about sharing personal information. Because of such complexities, the framing of an issue can "be pivotal in directing public opinion by making a case in favor of one of the two competing values" (Nelson 2004, 582). The Census Bureau spent millions of dollars to frame discussion of the census in terms of the positive benefits of cooperation. The Census Bureau assumed that the 2000 mobilization campaign would be a rare instance in which political leadership offered a unified message. This assumption held until the eruption of the privacy debate. Then, for a brief but critical period, political consensus about census cooperation broke down. The privacy debate offered a different and explicitly negative frame about the census, one that played to a public predisposed to mistrust an intrusive government. Thus, our analysis must do more than simply evaluate an information campaign; it must sort out the influence of the competing census frames that were pushed into public discourse. Do competing frames simply nullify one another, or does just one frame, perhaps the more intense one, shape mass opinion and behavior? The few works that have explicitly considered the effect of opposing frames have concluded that competing frames effectively cancel each other out (Brewer 2002; Druckman 2004; Sniderman and Theriault 2004). The unexpected privacy debate offers the opportunity to explore the influence of competing frames on census cooperation in the context of a real-world application.

Finally, our research contributes to the pervasive civic engagement literature. The decline in census cooperation in recent decades has often been viewed through the lens of the concurrent downward spiral in civic engagement in the late twentieth century.[4] Although the extent of the dire prognosis for American democracy remains the subject of considerable debate, scholars have linked civic engagement to a wide range of public goods, including a nation's prospects for effective, responsive self-government, individual development, and economic prosperity (Brehm and Rahn 1997; Fukuyama 1995; Inglehart 1999; Putnam 2000; Skocpol and Fiorina 1999). So, to the extent that census participation can be viewed as a civic activity, understanding census participation has implications for the health and prospects of our national civic life. In modeling the determinants of census participation, we explicitly evaluate the parallels between census participation and political participation, examining the impact of social capital on both. Thus, this analysis also considers the impact and importance of social capital and helps us answer the fundamental motivating question of why some individuals cooperate with the census and others do not, and whether such cooperation can be encouraged with a mobilization campaign.

DIFFICULTIES OF MEASURING MOBILIZATION

Before turning to the specifics of our research design, we should acknowledge and discuss one inherent difficulty of evaluating campaign effects that is conceptual in nature. How exactly do we define and measure the campaign? The way a campaign is operationalized and measured has a profound effect on our understanding of it and of its influence on the mass public. Indeed, much of the contemporary debate about campaign effects in political science and mass communications is focused on seemingly technical issues of methodological approach and variable measurement (Iyengar 2001). As we discuss in the next section, our study design recognizes these various conceptual and methodological issues.

One of the most common approaches to evaluating campaign effects is to rely on mass surveys. Historically, research attempted to assess the effect of a campaign by using a cross-sectional survey *after the campaign*. Political science survey research finds, for instance, that self-reported contact from a campaign correlates with voter turnout (Rosenstone and Hansen 1993). Unfortunately, the explicit link between contact and voter behavior cannot be confirmed with a one-shot survey because candidates often target contact to individuals who are already planning to vote. Surveys may be powerful tools for analyzing relationships at a given point in time, but a single survey cannot gauge attitudinal or behavioral change. Longitudinal studies, in which measures are repeatedly asked of different people, can track aggregate changes, but only a panel survey design, in which the same individuals are measured at different points in time, can link individual changes in attitude or behavior to campaign efforts. Although more common than in the past, longitudinal and panel surveys are considerably more expensive than conventional surveys, so the cross-sectional survey remains the norm in social science.

How campaign exposure is measured within the context of a survey has also been a source of debate. Self-reported exposure measures, in particular, have come under considerable scrutiny because of high levels of measurement error (Price and Zaller 1993). Simply asking respondents to guesstimate the number of advertisements they saw in the past week, in the past month, or during the entire campaign is an imprecise measure of campaign exposure. Indeed, research finding a relationship between self-reported advertising exposure and voter turnout has been dismissed because of the blunt and error-prone measurement of self-reported advertising exposure. Most notably, the people who best recall watching political advertisements are those who were already planning to vote (Bartels 1993).

Experimental studies are able to overcome such design problems with a more clearly delineated "campaign treatment," but experiments have their own problems and limitations. Although experiments allow researchers to isolate the influence of a specific treatment, they generally have limited external validity because they usually take place under artificial conditions. For instance, experimental research has also found that political advertisements have a considerable impact on turnout and candidate support (Ansolabehere and Iyengar 1995), but critics argue that these effects may be exaggerated because respondents are unnaturally attentive to the ads within the laboratory context, being unable to change the channel or make a run to the refrigerator during commercial breaks. And because experiments often use a nonrandom sample or geographically concentrated sample (such as students at a college), the experimental findings cannot be generalized and may be difficult to replicate (Finkel and Geer 1998).

How do we isolate the 2000 census campaign from other processes that were occurring in the society? Certainly mobilization efforts did not occur in a vacuum. At the height of the census advertising campaign, there were multiple sources of information—news stories, community leaders, jokes on late night TV. Some of these other sources were designed by the Census Bureau. In addition to the paid political advertising on TV and radio and in newspapers, the official campaign included an ambitious community partnerships program, a census-in-the-schools effort, and a church-based program. These and other efforts are incorporated into our measurements. The influence of other media attention—sometimes welcomed, sometimes not—is less amenable to direct measurement. The public relations director of the Census Bureau daily informed the director about press stories, not unlike the president getting a daily intelligence briefing. Even before the eruption of the privacy debate, there were negative stories—about delays in hiring, local office snafus, mayors' complaints that their city was being overlooked, mail delays, and what had gone wrong in the previous census—as if to tempt fate. The bureau regularly and forcefully responded to these stories, attempting to quiet any negative buzz and, of course, to promote spontaneous positive stories (of which there were hundreds during the census period).

The point, of course, is the impossibility of isolating the highly directed census mobilization from the swirl of public attention that an event as large as a census inevitably attracts. In this book, our approach is to analyze the role of the mobilization effort from as many angles as possible, employing a number of innovative methodologies. At times we measured the campaign by self-reported exposure to the census advertising campaign. Other times we asked respondents whether they recognized specific television ads. At still other times we showed the respondents a full video of a census ad. But ultimately we had to acknowledge that the campaign encompassed both what the Census Bureau could control and what it could not. Thus, for example, when we measured changes in opinions and attitudes over time, we were capturing all information about the census that individuals might receive—whether from their neighbors, a favorite news anchor, an angry talk show host, a union leader, or the Census Bureau itself. Though consistent with a number of other studies (Bartels 1993; Zaller 1992), this is, of course, a very broad definition of the census campaign.

Finally, we added to these various measurement strategies an experimental design in which we controlled the information that the respondents received about the census. Each of these approaches has strengths and weaknesses; taken together they offer broad evidence about the role of campaign efforts and the privacy debate in shaping census attitudes and cooperation.

DATA AND METHODOLOGY

We use several data sources in this book, but the core empirical analysis for each of the three data chapters comes from the Stanford Institute for the Quantitative Study of Society (SIQSS) census monitoring surveys, an innovative panel design conducted by Knowledge Networks and supported by a consortium of foundations.[5] (A public use data file is being prepared.)

Knowledge Networks (KN) maintains an Internet-based panel of a national sample of households, recruited by random-digit dialing (RDD), who either have been provided Internet access through their own computer or are given a WebTV console to connect to the Internet.[6] The KN sample is broadly representative of the U.S. population. Although the SIQSS monitoring surveys are conducted over the Internet, respondents are a probability sample of the U.S. population. By using a methodology that produces a representative sample of the U.S. population, KN overcomes the most common shortfall of previous Internet surveys. The viability of this methodological approach has been demonstrated in a number of objective comparison tests (Krosnick and Chang 2001; Viscusi, Huber, and Bell 2004).

SIQSS conducted a series of seven monitoring surveys from late February to early June 2000.[7] The series started with a baseline survey (February 25 to March 8) that gathered attitudinal, behavioral, and demographic data on the 9,064 panel members randomly selected from the KN panel. The first wave, completed well before census forms were mailed out (though not, as would have been preferable, before any census information was reported or advertised), made no reference to the census. It collected basic demographic data and responses to a long, detailed list of political and attitudinal measures that might be expected to be related to census cooperation. The baseline survey was completed by 7,344 respondents (81 percent completion rate). The survey instrument was designed with the classic studies of voting behavior and citizen participation in mind.

This initial baseline survey was followed by five monitoring surveys that started just as census forms were mailed and concluded when the census operation shifted from mail-out/mail-back to nonresponse follow-up, when the bureau sent enumerators to households from which no form had been received (March 3 to April 13). Each monitor consisted of a randomly selected, unique subsample of approximately one-fifth of the initial baseline sample (sampling done without replacement).[8] All monitors addressed issues relating to the mobilization campaign and the census in general, including items on privacy and confidentiality. Finally, a follow-up survey (June 5–6, 2000) was conducted from a random sample of baseline respondents. Of the 3,042 panelists from the baseline survey who were sent the follow-up survey, 2,413 completed the survey, for a 79 percent completion rate. The main objective of the follow-up survey was to collect information on the public's experience with the form itself. To this end, we asked an array of questions about how respondents answered the form and how they felt about specific questions or types of questions.

In total, respondents were interviewed a maximum of three times: first in the baseline survey before the census campaign, second in one of the monitors during the census campaign, and finally in the follow-up after the campaign. Such a data structure (combined longitudinal and panel survey) gives us an opportunity to evaluate the changes in census opinions over the course of the heightened census campaign, and much of our analysis focuses on the over-time dynamics.

When the privacy debate erupted in mid- to late March, we fielded two additional and separate surveys, each with a completely new sample of respondents so that there would be no overlap between respondents in the seven SIQSS monitoring surveys and these surveys. The first of these additional surveys was designed to gauge immediate exposure and reaction to the privacy debate. The second was a carefully designed experiment used to evaluate the impact of elite and media rhetoric on census cooperation. In total, then, our study draws on the monitoring surveys, a cross-sectional survey, and a specially designed experiment testing the impact of the privacy debate.

Since Internet-based surveys are a relatively new methodological approach, it is worth remarking on the benefits for our particular study. First, the technological capabilities of the methodology allowed us to go beyond standard self-reported recall of the campaign advertising. Although we measured exposure to the campaign using this traditional measure, we were also able to show still shots of actual ads as well as videos of full ads. We cannot overstate the benefits of this design. To incorporate video or pictures into a research project in the past, researchers typically gathered a group of respondents together in an unnatural setting, most often a college classroom. Such an approach casts serious doubts on the external validity of the research; beyond the inconvenience to the respondents (which might influence response rates), the sample is unlikely to be nationally representative, and watching a video in a college classroom with a room full of strangers is hardly equivalent to watching a TV in your own living room. In contrast, the surveys we conducted for this study, including the video and electronic picture components, took place in the home of the respondent at his or her convenience.

Over the course of our study, the panel component became more important than anticipated. In addition to assessing mobilization efforts, we were able to adapt to and measure the effects of the privacy debate that broke out and then peaked during the field periods of the census and our monitoring studies. Since the privacy debate erupted while we were already monitoring public attitudes toward the census, it created a quasi-natural experiment, which we were able to capture and measure. Finally, we gained considerable leverage over the effect of the privacy debate with an experimental design in which we administered some of the offending questions in the long form to members of our panel.

AN OUTLINE OF THE BOOK

In chapter 1, we provide a broad overview of the social and political context of the 2000 census count, discussing the general and often universal problems that have plagued accurate population counts throughout American history. We review why and how Census 2000 focused on two issues: first, reversing or at least stabilizing the historical decline in voluntary mail return of the census forms; and second, reducing the persistent and disproportionate undercount among poor and minority segments of the population. We discuss the many challenges the Census Bureau faced in attaining those goals and the motivations for the massive mobilization campaign.

In chapter 2, we describe the massive media and mobilization campaign that the Census Bureau developed to improve census cooperation, and we offer a rigorous empirical evaluation of its effect on census awareness, knowledge, attitudes, and cooperation. This public outreach effort, though designed to reach the entire population, was heavily targeted toward the population groups that historically have been the hardest to reach and have had the lowest participation rates—particularly African Americans, Hispanics, and recent immigrants. We find that the census campaign was enormously successful, especially among these targeted groups, and helped to increase knowledge about the census and voluntary mail-back cooperation. The pronounced impact of the campaign on census participation stands in stark contrast to the conclusions of decades of research on political and public health campaigns, which has been unable to link mobilization efforts directly to mass behavior, and it directly challenges the assumption of the knowledge gap literature that the campaign would fail to mobilize the hardest-to-count groups.

In chapter 3, we discuss the politics and background of the privacy debate and then empirically assess its effect on opinions about the census, census cooperation, and long-form completion. Using the monitoring studies, an experimental design, and a cross-sectional survey, we find compelling evidence that the privacy debate—a decidedly partisan information campaign—served to depress cooperation (although that effect was largely offset by the mobilization campaign) and encouraged item nonresponse among those receiving the census long form. This analysis offers a real-world evaluation of competing framing effects and suggests that conflicting messages can simultaneously influence public attitudes and behavior.

In chapter 4, we offer an empirical analysis and comparison of census participation and voter turnout, evaluating the similarities and differences between these different forms of civic engagement. This exercise reveals an interesting discovery: many of the community engagement characteristics long believed to predict both census cooperation and voting behavior in fact have little impact on the decision to complete a census form. Rather, it appears that more fundamental factors, such as household structure and family composition, better predict census participation. This finding challenges many of the long-standing assumptions of the Census Bureau and civic engagement scholars and has implications for future mobilization efforts.

Finally, in chapter 5, we discuss the policy implications of our findings, drawing out the consequences of our results for future censuses and other government surveys. Most notably, we discuss the enduring challenges that the Census Bureau will face in attempting to obtain a full and complete population count of the United States and we identify the emerging threats to our national statistical system.

Chapter One | The Social Context and the Political Climate

ON DECEMBER 28, 2000, the Census Bureau announced that on Census Day (April 1, 2000) the population of the United States had been precisely 281,421,906.[1] Although this number resulted from an impressive logistic operation and was the product of a complex counting process, it was just an estimate. The Census Bureau knew, as did any knowledgeable observer, that the "true count" was 281 million individuals—give or take a few million. No population census, in the United States or elsewhere, from biblical times to the modern era, is exact. No census operation can find and persuade everyone to cooperate or be certain that the final count does not include duplicates or erroneous enumerations.

Of this nation's first census, in 1790, President George Washington commented:

> Returns of the Census have already been made from several of the States and a tolerably just estimate has been formed now in others, by which it appears that we shall hardly reach four millions; but one thing is certain: our real numbers will exceed, greatly, the official returns of them; because the religious scruples of some would not allow them to give in their lists; the fear of others that it was intended as the foundation of a tax induced them to conceal or diminished theirs; and thro' the indolence of the people and the negligence of many of the Officers, numbers are omitted. (Fitzpatrick 1939, 329)

Take a close look at the reasons given by the nation's first president for what he claimed to be an undercount. Some among the population had scruples, suggested Washington, precluding their cooperation with the census. Others feared it would be used against them or expose them to government attention they hoped to avoid. Then there was simple indolence. We can give Washington's three reasons modern labels. The first would be principled objection to the very idea that government has a right to ask citizens who they are and where they live—in other words, a fundamental concern about privacy. The second reason Washington cites could be called confidentiality fears, although in the current era these individuals are more frequently illegal immigrants or criminals than tax evaders. And finally, indolence is known to us today as lack of civic engagement or indifference to civic obligation. President Washington was quick to add that it was not just the habits of the population that were at fault. Poor performance by census-takers—who were federal marshals in 1790—came in for their share of the blame.

The focus of this book is on the first set of reasons adduced by Washington: what is it in the habits, attitudes, and lifestyles of America's population that makes it difficult to enumerate everyone in the decennial census? And how do these characteristics interact with public dialogue about the census? Answers to these questions are critical to evaluating what the government can and cannot do to convince reluctant Americans to cooperate in the decennial count. Preparations are already well under way for the 2010 census, and the analysis here holds direct implications for the specific policies and procedures that will ensure a successful enumeration. Beyond the public policy implications, our analysis of the complex interaction of public discourse, individual attitudes, and civic behavior helps us to understand the determinants of civic participation in the United States.

We begin with an overview of the American census.

THE AMERICAN CENSUS

Since 1790, it has occurred every ten years, as the Constitution mandates. For the first century or so a temporary census office was established each decade by congressional action. This office recruited and supervised a small army of census-takers to go door to door asking whatever questions had been authorized by Congress. This basic design remained in place well into the twentieth century, even after a permanent Census Bureau was established in 1904.

At midcentury and shortly thereafter, there were two radical changes in census-taking. One was the introduction in 1950 of the long form. Although the chief purpose of the decennial census is to enumerate every resident at a specific address so that the apportionment of congressional seats will reflect differential population growth at ten-year intervals, once census-takers are in the field, there are low marginal costs to collecting additional information. Beginning in 1820, the census form expanded accordingly, going beyond the head count and the basic demographic traits of age, gender, and civil status (slave or free). These additional items included a count of noncitizens in each household and collected occupational data as well, enumerating the individuals engaged in agriculture, manufacturing, and commerce. Questions were frequently added and less often subtracted throughout the nineteenth century. By 1910, the census was asking thirty-four detailed questions, including education, health, place of birth, service in the Civil War, and marital status, in addition to occupation, age, sex, race, and more detailed questions on American Indians and Alaska natives.

In the 1930s, statisticians at the Census Bureau and elsewhere were beginning to work out the principles of modern population sampling theory. First used in unemployment surveys in response to a need for such data in the Roosevelt administration, sampling theory was first used in the decennial census in 1940. In order to ask the growing list of additional questions without burdening the entire population, special questions on socioeconomic status and housing conditions were asked of a 5 percent sample of the population.

By 1960, when for the first time the Census Bureau experimented with mailing out census forms to some households, sampling had matured into a two-form census. The short-form questions—name, age, date of birth, gender, race, relation to other household members, residency type (rental or owned), and the number of people in each household—were asked of everyone in the population. A long form with many more questions was sent to approximately one in six households.

The experimentation with mailing out some forms in 1960 led to an even more radical change in 1970. For nearly two centuries the census had been a face-to-face, door-to-door enumeration. This labor-intensive method was a costly way to track down America's mobile, far-flung, and busy population, especially after a large number of women joined the labor force and it became more difficult to find a household member at home. As a cost-control measure, the Census Bureau turned to a mail-out/mail-back design. In the 1960 census, households were instructed to keep the completed mail-out forms until they were picked up by an enumerator. In the 1970 census, for those households whose mailing address was their residence (not a post office box), the Census Bureau mailed the form with the instruction to complete it at home and mail it back to the bureau.

The Census Bureau quickly learned that a mail-out/mail-back census not only reduced costs but also improved data quality. One source of error in any survey is the interaction between the person asking questions and the person answering them. By removing possible misunderstandings or recording errors in this interaction, the census more accurately reflected population and housing conditions. The mail-out/mail-back census became the preferred design. In 2000, approximately 80 percent of America's households received the census via the post office. For households without postal delivery, a census employee delivered the form, leaving it to be mailed back in. About 1 percent of households were so remote that the census-taker had to revert to old-fashioned face-to-face enumeration. Our interest in this book is with the approximately 99 percent of households asked to return the census form by mail.

Not all did, which sets the central questions for our analysis.

THE MAIL-BACK RESPONSE RATE

When, in 1970, the census initiated the mail-out/mail-back design, some 78 percent of the population returned the form. This rate dropped slightly, to 75 percent, in the 1980 census, and then declined significantly in 1990, to 65 percent. In preparing for the census in 2000, the bureau initially feared a mail-back response rate as low as 55 percent.[2] Following extensive eval-uation research and modifications of previous strategies, the Census Bureau concluded that a 61 percent mail-back rate was a prudent target and bud-geted and staffed accordingly. We have more to say about the 2000 target later. At this point we simply emphasize that cooperation rates declined steadily from 1970 to 1990 and that there was every reason to expect that trend to continue in 2000 (see figure 1.1).

Figure 1.1   Census Response Rate, 1970 to 1990, and Projected Response Rate in 2000

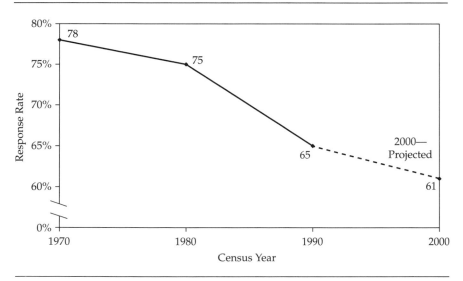

Source: U.S. Census Bureau (2000).

What might account for this precipitous decline in census cooperation? What could the Census Bureau do about it? What happened in the 2000 census? What do the results from 2000 tell us about census-taking in 2010 and beyond? These questions, which organize the analysis to follow, can be addressed only by first considering the complex interaction between the prevailing social climate and the political context as it influenced planning for the 2000 census. Central to this planning was a new approach to a long-standing issue—the census undercount.

For more than a half-century the Census Bureau had systematically evaluated its effort in the decennial census and, until 2000, consistently found a net undercount—it missed more persons than it erroneously included or double-counted. (In 2000, as discussed in chapter 5, it reported an over-count.)[3] To be sure, the United States is not alone in finding that it undercounts its population in a census. China, in its 2000 census, reported an undercount of nearly 23.6 million individuals (approximately 2 percent of the population), a sharp increase from the prior census. The increase in China was attributed to growing privacy concerns and a large and elusive migrant worker population. The 2001 census in the United Kingdom similarly reported an undercount of approximately 2 percent, which was attributed to a young and mobile population as well as a large number of asylum seekers and immigrants who avoided the census.

The questions of how to estimate the undercount and whether to use adjusted population figures to correct for it were at the center of a fierce political controversy in the lead-up to the 2000 U.S. census. The issue at the heart of this controversy is that the population groups most likely to be undercounted are disproportionately racial and ethnic minorities living in central cities. Insofar as members of this group are politically active, they are more likely to vote Democratic than Republican. Consequently, when the Census Bureau focuses on the undercounted population groups, which it must do to meet its obligation to include as close to 100 percent of the population as possible, it runs the risk of being charged with having a partisan agenda. This in fact was what happened in the lead-up to the census in 2000. But the charge was mistaken: the Census Bureau had (and has) no partisan agenda. But it is not difficult to see why Republican congressional leaders thought differently.

A complex interaction links demographic realities, census cooperation rates, the census undercount and efforts to reduce it, and perceived partisan advantages. As suggested by this chapter's title, there was a social-demographic context *and* a political-partisan climate that jointly affected the taking of the census in 2000 and the possibility that an improved cooperation rate in the mail-back phase would contribute to reducing the census undercount.

THE SOCIAL CONTEXT OF THE CENSUS IN 2000

A census is a statistical description of the nation's population, but this population is made up of many different groups that vary in how easy they are to find as well as in how willing they are to cooperate. In the previous section, we noted that China complained about an elusive migrant worker population that was difficult to enumerate, and the United Kingdom cited a rise in the number of asylum seekers and immigrants and a generally more mobile population in explaining its census undercount. Similar patterns hold in the United States, where the Census Bureau is well aware of certain "hard-to-count" population groups: the geographically mobile, renters, the unemployed, recent immigrants, and illegal aliens. It also has a list of the demographic groups most likely to be double-counted: college students, persons with two homes, and children of separated parents with joint custody. Because our concern is voluntary census cooperation, especially in the mail-out/mail-back phase of the census, we do not focus on the groups that are double-counted or otherwise erroneously included in the census.[4]

The first contextual hurdle facing the Census Bureau is the basic reality that the demographic groups that are harder to count and historically least likely to cooperate with the census constitute a growing proportion of the population. To approach its target of 100 percent coverage, the Census Bureau has to run harder just to stay in place.

Immigrants and Minorities: A Growing Proportion of the Population

The United States is rivaled only by Canada in its claim to have the most racially and ethnically diverse population in the world, a result of its long, continuous history as a nation of immigrants. Of course, population diversity—a term not easily defined—precedes even the great immigrant flows of the nineteenth century. At the moment of the nation's founding, 20 percent of America's population included five hundred Native Indian tribal groups and Africans from dozens of different ethnicities and linguistic groups, representing diversity far greater than that which differentiated northern Europeans into their Protestant sects and national-origin groupings.

The diversity narrative, however, is largely viewed from the perspective of the nineteenth and early twentieth centuries, and then again the latter decades of the twentieth century. The nineteenth-century story is about both territorial expansion and immigration. The purchase of the Louisiana Territory from France added Creoles to the base population. The purchase of the Russian colony of Alaska in 1867 added the Inuit, the Kodiak, and other Alaskan natives. The Mexican-American War in midcentury added the nation's first large Mexican population, about eighty thousand people. The Spanish-American War later in the century added Puerto Rico, other Caribbean islands and their peoples, Guam, and the Philippines. When Hawaii was annexed in 1898, its native Pacific Islander population fell under American governance. Although the population increases that resulted from conquest and purchase were relatively small, they added substantially to the country's ethno-racial diversity.

The massive flow of nineteenth-century immigrants added Germans, Scandinavians, and Irish to the Anglo base, and then the southern and eastern Europeans—Poles, Hungarians, and Italians. These immigrant flows represented a religious shift as well as one of national origins. Catholics and Jews joined the nation's founding Protestant base. In the 1960s, reform of immigration policy dramatically shifted the source of new immigrants from Europe to Asia and Latin America. The United States is now a pan-world nation.

One practical consequence of such demographic changes is the challenge to census-taking. No doubt immigrants in the nineteenth century—Irish in crowded city tenement housing, Chinese labor in mining camps—were less accurately counted than other demographic groups, but statistical science was too primitive then to estimate undercounts, let alone undercounts in specific demographic groups. We now better understand how census enumeration is complicated by factors such as language and cultural differences and the fact that minority communities and immigrants live in hard-to-count areas such as inner-city neighborhoods, barrios, remote rural areas, and reservations. Such areas are often characterized by crowded housing conditions, and residents may be hesitant to cooperate with a census if they have more relatives or renters living with them than are allowed under their leases.

The proportion of people in the United States who are "hard to count" increased between 1990 and 2000, one of the factors that led the Census Bureau to expect cooperation in the mail-back phase of the census to be lower in 2000 than in 1990. Figure 1.2 illustrates the population growth among ethnic and racial minorities in the decades leading up to the 2000 census. The single largest growing minority population in the United States is the Hispanic population, one of the most undercounted communities in the country. Although only 6.4 percent of the population identified themselves as being of Hispanic origin in 1980, the first year when the census collected comparable data, that number increased to 12.5 percent in 2000, and the number is projected to nearly double by the year 2050. The Asian and Pacific Islander proportion of the population has also increased

Figure 1.2   Racial Minorities Based on the U.S. Census,
              1970 to 2000

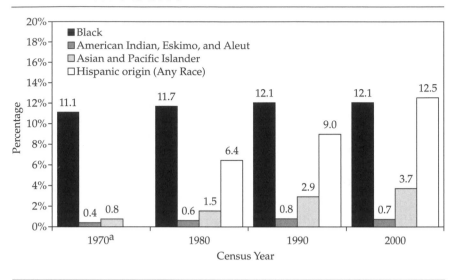

Source: U.S. Census Bureau, http://www.census.gov/population/www/documentation / twps0056.html.
Note: The percentage of whites in the total population declined from 87.5 percent in 1970 to 75.1 percent in 2000.
[a] Hispanic origin was consistently collected by the census beginning in 1980.

dramatically—from less than 1 percent of the population in 1970 to nearly 4 percent in 2000. In contrast, the African American proportion of the population has remained relatively stable in recent decades.

From the perspective of census-taking, recent immigrants pose special difficulties. Persons not born in the United States, especially if they are here illegally, are particularly reluctant to cooperate with the census. In addition to language barriers, there is lack of familiarity with the census and often a fear that their answers will be shared with the Immigration and Naturalization Service (INS). Even those who are in the United States legally are less apt to cooperate if they have recently arrived from countries with authoritarian governments or if they have little basis on which to willingly volunteer information to government officials. And of course, there are language barriers. Although the census forms in 2000 were printed in English, Spanish, Chinese, Vietnamese, Korean, and Tagalog (a language of the Philippines) and census help was provided in many additional languages, in fact more than one hundred languages are spoken in the United States.

As shown in figure 1.3, the number of foreign-born individuals in the United States increased from 9.6 million in 1970 to more than 31 million in 2000. Between 1990 and the census in 2000, the estimated number of illegal immigrants doubled, from 3.5 million to 7 million (see figure 1.4). High rates of immigration increased the proportion of individuals who had difficulty with English, from 4.8 percent in 1980 to 8.1 percent in 2000, as shown in table 1.1. Clearly, the hardest-to-count portion of the population was dramatically increasing in the years leading up to the 2000 census. And this was not the only challenge the Census Bureau faced in stemming the declining census response rate.

America's Changing Attitudes

President Washington complained about the indolence of the people, citing it as one reason the 1790 census result was lower than anticipated and, in his judgment, lower than the true number. As it prepared for the census in 2000, the Census Bureau was likewise concerned that prevailing civic attitudes in the population would drop cooperation rates below the already low rate experienced in 1990.

Figure 1.3   Foreign-Born Population in the United States, 1970 to 2000

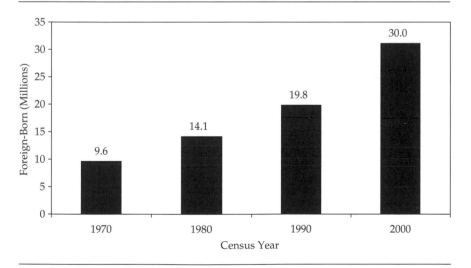

Source: Current Population Survey March supplement.

Figure 1.4   Estimated Unauthorized Immigrant Population in the
United States, 1990 to 2000

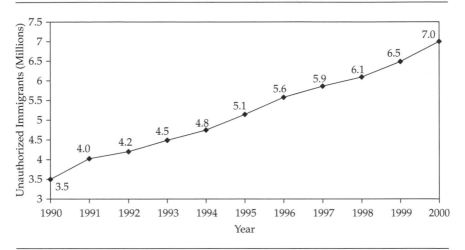

Source: Immigration and Naturalization Service, http://www.immigration.gov/graphics
/aboutus/statistics/Ill_Report_1211.pdf.
Note: The Census Bureau estimates that there were 8.7 million unauthorized immigrants in
the United States in 2000.

Table 1.1   Self-Reported English-Speaking Ability Among U.S.
Residents Age Five and Older, 1980, 1990, and 2000

Year	U.S. Residents Speaking English with Some Difficulty[a]	Percentage of Total Population	Percentage Change in Absolute Numbers Compared to Last Decade
1980	10,181,036	4.8	
1990	13,982,502	6.1	37.3
2000	21,320,407	8.1	52.5

Source: U.S. Census Bureau.
[a]Includes all persons who report speaking English less than "very well," the threshold for
full proficiency in English as determined by the U.S. Department of Education.

DECLINING RESPONSE RATES

In the period leading up to the 2000 census, the bureau had been tracking the three-decade decline in census mail-back cooperation as part of a much broader decline in survey responses throughout the survey research industry over the same period. There is no lack of evidence on steadily declining survey response rates.[5] Time pressure, technology, and privacy concerns are all forces converging on the American survey research industry that discourage consumers from taking the time to participate in studies. This secular decline stretching across the last several decades has affected all surveys, irrespective of sponsorship or content. Though government surveys have experienced less dramatic declines than surveys sponsored by academic institutions, and academically sponsored surveys in turn have been less hard hit than commercial firms, no survey sponsors have been immune. The preeminent university-sponsored survey of political attitudes and behavior experienced more than a fifteen-percentage-point decline in response rates between 1970 and 2000, when it fell to 60.5 percent.[6] And marketing firms settle for much lower cooperation rates. The Marketing Research Association estimates that the average survey cooperation rate for marketing surveys hovers around 25 percent.

Prestigious government surveys show similar if less dramatic declines. One of the nation's most important health surveys, conducted by the Centers for Disease Control and Prevention (CDC), has experienced a response rate drop from approximately 65 percent in the late 1980s to less than 50 percent at present.[7] Response rate declines are true of establishment surveys as well as population surveys. The all-important Economic Census, conducted by the Census Bureau every five years, collects data from corporations, partnerships, sole proprietorships, and other organizations with employees, representing 96 percent of the nation's economic activity. Although, like the decennial, this is a mandatory census, the nonresponse rate reached nearly 16 percent in 2002—a historic high. And the Census of Governments is experiencing nonresponse rates almost twice that rate—29.7 percent did not respond to the 2002 Local Government Directory Survey.

Both the government and private-sector research firms are driven to compensate in costly ways, such as making presurvey contacts, conducting repeated follow-up visits and telephone calls, and sometimes offering financial incentives. Timothy Triplett (2002) shows that the average number of call attempts by the Survey Research Center at the University of Maryland to complete an interview in a national survey has increased 30 percent (54 percent in statewide surveys) since 1989. These efforts might work up to a point, but they cannot overcome the two major sources of declining response rates: people are harder to reach, and when reached, they are more likely to refuse to cooperate. Of course, it is not easy to sort out the hard-to-reach from the refusals because some people "refuse" by making it impossible to reach them. They have unlisted phones or caller ID, and they don't take calls, not even from the Census Bureau. Thus, to some extent the bureau in 2000 was concerned about issues that had become commonplace in the survey industry.

Refusal rates have increased in part because there are now more opportunities to refuse, given the veritable explosion in direct marketing approaches disguised as "research." In the last decade, expenditures on direct mail have doubled, from $22 billion to $45 billion, and the proportion of mail attributed to direct advertising is now about one-half of all household mail. Although we have no firm estimate of the proportion of advertising mail and telemarketing calls that come disguised as questionnaires, experience indicates that it is substantial. Certainly many people do not distinguish between legitimate surveys and marketing disguised as surveys. A 2003 Council for Marketing and Opinion Research (CMOR) study finds that "selling under the guise of research" (known as SUGGING) has declined since the implementation of the "do not call" legislation in 2003, but it was a considerable problem for survey researchers in the time leading up to the 2000 census (CMOR 2003).

Figure 1.5 presents trends in public attitudes toward advertising mail from 1987 to 2000. Over a thirteen-year period, the proportion of the public preferring less advertising mail climbed from one-third to one-half. Research by the U.S. Postal Service finds a steady drop in the number of people who bother to read advertising or promotional mail; by 2000 that proportion was down to 12 percent.

Intrusive telemarketing has similar characteristics. It often masquerades as an informational survey. The public has angrily reacted, leading to the national "do not call" legislation and prompting call blocking devices such as caller ID and the now ubiquitous HUDI (hang up during introduction). An industry survey found that nearly three out of five respondents reported using their answering machine to screen calls, and one-third used caller ID.[8] Perhaps even more telling is that this survey itself reported a 60 percent refusal rate! New technologies may prevent individuals from receiving telemarketing phone calls, but they also block legitimate commercial, academic, and government telephone surveys.

The issue of interest here is whether saturating American households with information requests contributes to a growing weariness, or maybe wariness, that expresses itself as "leave me alone, I want my privacy," and whether this sentiment increases survey refusal rates and, consequently, census cooperation. Research has found that the most common reasons given for refusing to participate in surveys are "too busy/lack of time,"

Figure 1.5   Attitudes Toward Advertising Mail, 1987 to 2000

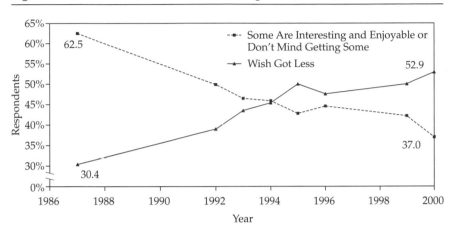

Source: U. S. Postal Service Household Diary Study, 1987 to 2000.
Note: Responses "Wish got more," "Don't know," "No answer," and "Received no advertising" are not shown. The percentage of those who wish they would get more advertising mail remains rather constant over the years in the range of 5.0 and 7.1 percent.

leading to a "leave me alone" attitude (O'Connor 1991). Such privacy concerns are also made apparent by the increased use of barriers to screen out "intrusive" outsiders. Those who can afford it often choose to live in gated communities or behind doormen instructed to block entry into apartment buildings. Unlisted phone numbers are another indicator: nearly 30 percent of U.S. households have at least one nonlisted or nonpublished telephone number (Survey Sampling 2001). In chapter 3, we examine the connection between increased public concern about privacy and confidentiality and respondent suspicion and mistrust about all surveys, whether government-sponsored or not. Not only are respondents suspicious about the legitimacy of a survey, but even if the survey is legitimate, many respondents believe it to be intrusive and are skeptical about the promise of confidentiality. These doubts played a major role in Census 2000.

DECLINING CIVIC PARTICIPATION

In addition to a declining willingness to participate in research and government surveys, American society has been marked by a more general decline in civic participation. Across a broad front, there has been a decline in civic participation over the past thirty years. Robert Putnam (1995, 2000), for instance, has reported that organizational membership has been in steady decline for several decades. Voting in presidential elections has shown similar trends (Rosenstone and Hansen 1993).[9] Declining civic participation can also affect census cooperation, particularly if the census is viewed as a civic responsibility and not just an information survey. In other words, even if a household distinguishes between a marketing scheme and a census form, cooperation is far from assured.

Similarly, trends in the public's trust in government have also been in decline since the 1950s. The public's trust in government is generally accepted as a further indicator of reluctance to cooperate with even the decennial census, perhaps because of concerns about confidentiality. Even at its highest level during the decade preceding the 2000 census, only 44 percent of the American public, according to the General Social Survey (GSS), reported trusting the government "some or most" of the time. Again, the trend was not reassuring for a census that is expected to enumerate 100 percent of the population.

The demographic, attitudinal, and participatory trends leading up to the 2000 census created a social context that was inhospitable, if not downright hostile, to a successful census enumeration. In subsequent chapters, we see how the planning for the census took into account the bleak social trends briefly summarized here. First, however, we turn to the impact of the political climate in the 1990s on key design decisions in the planning of Census 2000.

THE POLITICAL CLIMATE OF THE CENSUS IN 2000

A census occurs in a political as well as a social climate. Although probably no decennial census in American history has been completely free of calculations about how its results might advance one or another political interest, the political climate surrounding Census 2000 was unprecedented in intensity, visibility, and partisan hostility. Census design decisions were attacked as unconstitutional, twice argued before the Supreme Court, continuously and sharply scrutinized by Congress and other government agencies, made the subject of a steady stream of party-line votes and even a presidential veto, and inspired dozens of professional and advocacy groups to "choose sides" (Prewitt 2003/2005, 18–24).

Census numbers have always had political consequences. Following the 1790 census, for instance, George Washington used the first veto in American history to reject an apportionment formula advanced by Alexander Hamilton in favor of one written by Thomas Jefferson.[10] There were also very clear political consequences for including nonvoting slaves in early censuses, and thereby congressional apportionment, as it gave slave states additional electors in the Electoral College and increased their number of members of the U.S. House of Representatives relative to their voting populations. Another remarkable chapter in the politics of census numbers occurred after the 1920 census, when Congress refused to reapportion for a decade. Southern and rural interests in Congress had taken note that the 1920 census recorded the massive wartime population movement from the rural southern states to industrial northern cities, already home to politically radical immigrants and labor organizers. Congressional bickering over the reapportionment formula effectively blocked a reapportionment that would shift power from rural to urban America, now for the first time home to a majority of the population. Congress was not reapportioned until after the 1940 census. (For a detailed discussion, see Anderson 1988, 147–57.)

The politics impinging on the 2000 census was in some respects a continuation of these earlier episodes, being primarily about the allocation of power in a territorially based system of political representation. The major difference, however, was a much greater focus in 2000 on how the census *would be taken*, not just on how the census results would be applied. It is this difference that bears on the analysis presented in subsequent chapters, and so we pause here to summarize.

Every decennial census redistributes political power in line with the population shifts and differential rates of growth from one census to the next. When the results from the 2000 census were announced, for example, ten states lost congressional seats, with New York and Pennsylvania each losing two. Four fast-growing states—Arizona, Florida, Georgia, and Texas—each gained two seats, and four other states each gained one seat. Dramatically and instantly, the census-based reapportionment reduced the political power of the northern industrial states and increased it in the South and the West. There are implications for presidential elections as well, because regional strength in congressional seats carries over into the Electoral College. The allocation of congressional seats based on rates of population growth or decline is known as "reapportionment," a term often paired with "redistricting," which is the redrawing of congressional district boundaries within each state. Under a Supreme Court ruling familiarly known as the "one-person, one-vote principle," congressional districts must be drawn to be nearly identical in population size.[11] Because of population shifts from one census to the next, many congressional districts have to change their boundaries. To achieve the precision required by the Supreme Court ruling, block-by-block census numbers are used. This practice has now been carried down to other election areas—such as those from which state legislators, county commissioners, and city councilors are selected—though for state and local districts the requirement of mathematical precision is somewhat relaxed. The Voting Rights Act of 1965 carried the argument further. Whereas the Court in Wesberry v. Sanders was remedying inequality by population size, the Voting Rights Act remedied inequality in the voting opportunities afforded to minorities. In a series of legal and legislative acts that amended and extended the Voting Rights Act, the principle of nondiscriminatory results in redistricting was firmly established. If a minority group can demonstrate that it had less opportunity than other members of the electorate to elect representatives of its choice, it can sue to have the redistricting plan rejected (National Conference of State Legislatures 1999).

Federal census results determine whether the principles embedded in Wesberry v. Sanders and the Voting Rights Act are honored, and it was this pressure more than anything else that set the stage for the unprecedented political battles over the 2000 census. Still at issue was the question of whether all groups in society were fully included in the census, even though it had become clear by the 1960s that they were not—that African Americans were less likely to be fully counted than whites.

The visionary social scientist Daniel Patrick Moynihan, later a senator from New York, was the guiding hand behind the 1967 "Conference on Social Statistics and the City," which drew out the obvious implication:

> Where a group defined by racial or ethnic terms, and concentrated in special political jurisdictions is significantly undercounted in relation to other groups, then individual members of that group are thereby deprived of the constitutional right to equal representation in the House of Representatives and, by inference, in other legislative bodies. They are also deprived of their entitlement to partake in federal and other programs designed for areas and populations with their characteristics. In other words, miscounting the population could unconstitutionally deny minorities political representation or protection under the Voting Rights Act. It could also deny local jurisdictions grant funds from federal programs. (Heer 1968, 11)

This conference linked the politics of the civil rights era with the technical work under way at the Census Bureau on what it labeled the "differential undercount."

Although census professionals had long presumed that there were errors in the census count, and that they probably netted out in the negative, it was not until the latter half of the twentieth century that statistical practice was advanced enough to estimate the census undercount. The initial breakthrough was the by-product of the universal selective service draft registration instituted when the United States responded to the attack on Pearl Harbor. Universal registration gave statisticians two independent estimates of the number of American males between the ages of twenty-one and thirty-five—

one reported in the 1940 census and the other from military records. Comparing these two numbers provided the first reliable estimate of how many persons, at least among young males, were missed in the census.

This comparison indicated an undercount in the 1940 census of approximately 3 percent, a figure that was not surprising to demographers and statisticians. Initially this census fact attracted little interest beyond technical circles. But with civil rights pressures coming to the foreground in the 1950s and then, explosively, in the 1960s, one feature of the undercount gained wide prominence. African American males of draft age had been missed in the 1940 census at more than four times the rate for whites. Here was the first systematic evidence of a census undercount that penalized African Americans.

As this definitive demonstration of the *differential undercount* gained political currency in the turbulent 1970s, pressure on the Census Bureau increased as it prepared for the 1980 census. After all, the census was constitutionally established to ensure that political power and representation would be equitably allocated, and enumerating some groups more completely than others put equal treatment at risk.

What should or could the Census Bureau do about the increasingly unacceptable differential undercount? There were two possibilities. The first was to conduct a traditional census more effectively—that is, to "count better." As part of this effort, the bureau introduced various coverage improvement methods, including more advertising to increase cooperation, an increase in the number of multilingual census-takers who could reach out to hard-to-count population groups, and multiple callbacks to nonresponding households. These improvements did begin to reduce the overall undercount from one census to the next, but the differential undercount between whites and African Americans persisted.

It was in this context that the Census Bureau turned to a second approach to tackling the differential undercount: the statistically innovative and controversial tactic of dual system estimation. The idea is simple (though the execution is not!). The Census Bureau takes the census and nearly simultaneously conducts a large sample survey, using block listing and implementation procedures independent of and indeed insulated from the census operation.[12] The independent sample survey offers a second population count that is compared with the census; the statistical properties of dual system estimation allow statisticians to adjust the raw census counts to align them more accurately with the true size of different population groups. Specifically, and most importantly, it corrects for differences in how well African Americans were counted compared to whites. (For an extensive technical discussion, see Citro et al. 2004.)

The first major test of dual system estimation in the census environment took place in 1980. The Census Bureau evaluated the results and concluded that problems in the design and execution precluded statistically reliable adjustment.[13] It announced that there would be no adjustment of the 1980 census, but promised that it would continue its statistical work on dual system estimation in anticipation of adjusting the next census in 1990. (For detail on both the 1980 and 1990 legal and political disputes, see Anderson and Fienberg 1999.)

This promise did not satisfy some political groups, who believed the rights of minorities were being denied by the census undercount. Technical problems notwithstanding, these interests wanted dual system estimation applied. More than fifty lawsuits were filed seeking to require the adjustment of the 1980 census to compensate for missed minorities and city dwellers. The most serious legal challenge, brought by Detroit, New York City, and New York State, sought to stop the release of the 1980 census results until they were adjusted. Under court order, the results were released on schedule, but the case was allowed to proceed to trial. A court ruling eventually upheld the Census Bureau's decision because it had not acted in an "arbitrary and capricious" manner.

During the 1980s the bureau continued its statistical work, convinced that there was a good chance that adjustment methods could be used in the 1990 census. It planned accordingly.

By now, however, it was naive to presume that census planning could be insulated from partisan politics. Because the Republican and Democratic Parties were roughly balanced, even very small changes in re-apportionment and redistricting could decide which political party controlled the Congress or the White House. The "one-person, one-vote" ruling of the Supreme Court put pressure on the parties to squeeze every possible advantage out of the redrawing of congressional districts after the 1990 census. Increasingly sophisticated computer-assisted methods allowed the parties to make fine-grained decisions down to the block level.

In this strongly partisan environment, the Census Bureau announced in mid-decade that the 1990 census would include a post-enumeration survey and that the raw census data, barring technical difficulties, would be adjusted to minimize the differential undercount. The Commerce Department, which has formal authority over the Census Bureau, rejected the bureau's plan. The department was quickly taken to court by a coalition of local governments and advocacy groups insisting that the plan be reinstated. An out-of-court settlement allowed the Census Bureau to include a post-enumeration survey in the 1990 census design, but then gave to the Secretary of Commerce the authority to set the criteria by which its results would be evaluated and to make the final decision about whether the raw census results would be adjusted.

To understand why the Commerce Department tried to stop its own bureau from designing the 1990 census as it saw fit, it is important to note that census methods had shaded into partisan politics. By the time of the 1990 census, it was obvious that among the population groups consistently undercounted were urban minorities, while those most likely to be over-counted were predominantly suburban white families with college students or weekend homes. Leaders in the Democratic Party understandably wanted a census method that would increase urban populations because urban populations are more likely to elect Democratic candidates. Thus, the Democratic Party believed that eliminating the undercount would favor Democratic interests. Republican Party strategists, also understandably, were therefore opposed to changing the traditional census.

Both sides dressed their arguments about census methods in high-minded language. Democrats spoke of fairness, not partisan advantage. They insisted that the bureau be allowed to apply whatever scientific methods it thought would improve census accuracy. Republicans cited the constitutional provision that an "actual enumeration" be taken as reason to reject any plan using sampling, and they argued that there was no guarantee of a more accurate census using sampling and dual system estimation. Both sides found support among reputable statisticians, though the weight of professional judgment favored the bureau's adjustment design.

Leading up to the 1990 census, it had been a Republican secretary of Commerce who tried but was unable to stop the bureau from including a post-enumeration sample survey. The subsequent out-of-court settlement produced a curious directive: the bureau would execute the census, evaluate its work, and then decide whether adjustment would improve the raw count—but its decision would take the form of a recommendation to the Secretary who had opposed the design in the first place. This set the stage for a confrontation—and that is what happened with the 1990 census.

The Census Bureau's statisticians concluded that dual system estimation had worked well enough to warrant statistical adjustment. Barbara Bryant, director of the bureau and a Republican appointee, agreed with this conclusion and presented her recommendation to Secretary Robert A. Mosbacher. (See the lively account in Bryant and Dunn 1995.) He rejected the recommendation. Overruling a statistical agency in this way was unprecedented, and so was one of the reasons given by the secretary for his decision:

> The choice of the adjustment method selected by the Census Bureau officials can make a difference in apportionment, and the political outcome of that choice can be known in advance. I am confident that political considerations played no role in the Census Bureau's choice of an adjustment model for the

1990 census. I am deeply concerned, however, that adjustment would open the door to political tampering with the census in the future. (Mosbacher 1991)[14]

This is the first time in American history that a high government official voiced the charge that the nonpartisan, professionally managed Census Bureau might choose a data collection methodology in order to favor one political party over another. The secretary's language was cautious, and he was careful to say that it could happen, not that it had. But in the highly charged political atmosphere, cautionary language was soon forgotten. In the close presidential election of 1992, Arkansas governor Bill Clinton defeated the incumbent Republican, George H. W. Bush. Republicans felt that an outsider, and an untrustworthy one at that, had captured the White House. Partisan polarization reached new highs in the 1994 congressional elections, which brought to Congress a number of conservative Republicans deeply mistrustful of Clinton. The Republican Party gained control of the House of Representatives in 1994 and kept control during the entire period in which the 2000 census was planned and fielded.

Unfortunately, but inevitably, census design became a target of partisan animosities. Statistical adjustment, often though inaccurately reduced to the label "sampling," became a political football. The Democratic Party, with its control of the White House, had no doubt that the census could improve its political fortunes. The Secretary of Commerce was the politically well-connected Bill Daley, son of the renowned Chicago mayor Richard Daley. Mayor Daley, of course, was remembered by Republicans as the party boss who had "stolen" the election that barely sent Kennedy to the White House three decades earlier. Republicans were deeply distrustful of what they saw as a political Commerce Department, and certainly the department forcefully protected the Census Bureau's right to prepare a 2000 census that incorporated the adjustment methodology.

Congressional Republicans were now in control of the key subcommittees that reviewed the census plans. Their position was clear: in 1997, Jim Nicholson, chairman of the Republican National Committee (RNC), sent the following call to arms to party leaders:

I am contacting you to recruit your assistance in addressing an issue of unusual importance to the future of Republican Party. At the heart of the matter is one of the federal government's most fundamental Constitutional functions: the United States census. At stake is our GOP majority in the House of Representatives, as well as partisan control of state legislatures nationwide.

The Clinton Administration is implementing a radical new way of taking the next census that effectively will add nearly four and one-half million

Democrats to the nation's population. This is the political outcome of a controversial Executive decision to use a complex mathematical formula to estimate and "adjust" the 2000 census. . . .

The GOP would suffer a negative effect in the partisan makeup of 24 Congressional seats, 113 State Senate seats and 297 State House seats nationwide. . . . An adjusted census could provide Democrats the crucial edge needed to prevail in close contests to control several state legislative chambers.[15]

This prediction about the number of Republican seats that would be "lost" was never documented or subjected to independent analysis. Most students of reapportionment and redistricting believe that it is probably impossible a priori to calculate partisan shifts in legislatures resulting from a decennial census, and they would consider the predictions in this memo highly implausible. Plausibility, however, was not the issue. If the Republicans thought an adjustment design would hurt their interests, Democrats were just as certain that it would help theirs. Civil rights organizations argued in favor of the adjustment methodology, claiming that the Republican Party did not care about racial minorities and social justice. The Congressional Black Caucus—all Democrats—took up the census as a leading civil rights issue, and they were often joined by Hispanic and Asian American members of Congress. Dozens of congressional votes taken on census issues in the 1990s split on party lines.

One hardly surprising consequence of this partisanship was an unprecedented layer of official oversight and ongoing scrutiny of the Census Bureau. It was in the oversight system that the two political parties, one with control of the Congress and the other with control of the White House, jockeyed for advantage. This oversight took a number of different forms.

The most sustained oversight was provided by Congress, whose responsibilities trace to the Constitution: the census is to be carried out "in such Manner as [Congress] shall by Law direct." A number of committees and subcommittees with jurisdiction over one aspect or another of the census held hearings. In 1999 and 2000, the House Subcommittee on the Census held seventeen formal hearings on census plans and progress in which Republican members challenged the bureau's sampling strategies and the Democratic members just as vigorously defended it.

In addition, as part of a compromise reached during legal and budgetary battles over the census in 1998, Congress and the White House agreed to jointly appoint a Census Monitoring Board—the first of its kind in census history. This eight-person board, evenly divided between Republicans and Democrats, had its own professional staff and budget ($3 million). Its task, as its name implies, was to monitor the census, hold hearings, inspect census operations, make recommendations, and periodically issue reports on how it thought the census was going. Because the board was evenly divided along party lines, few joint reports were issued. The Republican side issued reports that worried about the possibility that the bureau would rely on sampling rather than work hard to count everyone, and the Democratic side issued reports that generally defended the census design and the performance of the bureau.

The Census Bureau also had its own collection of eight different advisory committees, which held a total of twenty-five meetings from mid-1998 to mid-2000. Five of these committees—those representing African Americans, Asians, Hispanics, American Indians, and Native Hawaiians/Pacific Islanders—focused sharply on the differential undercount issues and defended the sampling design. Other advisory groups, such as one from the National Academy of Sciences, focused on technical issues, particularly on how to improve statistical adjustment methodology.

Although the 2000 census, like all censuses, had multiple tasks and purposes, the focus of many of these different advisory and oversight groups was on only one of these purposes—to reduce the undercount and its differential consequences for racial groups. The impetus for this focus came from within as well as outside the Census Bureau. Within the bureau, professional pride had been wounded by the charge that 1990 was a "failed" census because the net undercount had increased. More tellingly, for a half-century the bureau had worked to understand the differential undercount well enough to fix it, thus far without success. It prepared for the 2000 census confident that sampling methodology could solve the undercount problem.[16]

Politics also contrived to make the undercount the centerpiece of the census design. An active coalition speaking for historically undercounted groups—Asians, Hispanics, and American Indians as well as African Americans—declared the undercount to be the "civil rights issue of the decade." Leaders of states and cities with high undercount rates in 1990 insisted that they had lost huge amounts of federal funds as a result, and they did not want a repeat in 2000. Both political parties, each for its own reasons, put the undercount at the center of their divergent strategies for taking the census. Even groups and interests that were less political—a huge and varied group of data users—wanted an accurate census, which they took to be one that would reduce the undercount.

From all sides the pressure mounted. The Census Bureau could approach the challenge of reducing the undercount in two ways: improving traditional census methods and making statistical adjustments using dual system estimation. In the world of census methods, this is not an either/or choice. There could be a full-scale application of traditional methods and also an application of the adjustment methodology if the effort fell short. The political world, however, did see the choice as either/or. The Republicans said no to adjustment, irrespective of how well traditional census methods enumerated different groups in the population. The Democrats held that the undercount was so resistant to traditional methods that only statistical adjustment could ensure fairness.

These predetermined, strongly held partisan positions ruled out what, in effect, political leadership had said in earlier times: "We expect the most accurate census possible and instruct the Census Bureau to use its experience and scientific judgment to select and administer a census design that has the highest probability of accuracy." That was not the message. With the partisan wrangling surrounding the 2000 census, there was no single message, only contradictory instructions.

Following a number of political maneuvers and a key Supreme Court case, the census in 2000 was a mixture of a much strengthened traditional census and the possible application of dual system estimation to redistricting, though not to reapportionment. It is not the task of this book to explore how this resolution came to be or to analyze what eventually transpired (for discussion, see Prewitt 2003/2005), but to focus more specifically on how the political climate affected cooperation rates with the census.

It did so in two ways. First, the political climate provided the funds and motivation to conduct the most ambitious traditional census ever, with an especially well-funded public outreach and civic mobilization campaign. Second, the partisanship surrounding the census interacted with an unexpected public outcry about the census as an invasion of privacy. We explore the effect of both of these messages about the census in chapters 2 and 3.

CONCLUSION

Every census, including its achieved level of accuracy and coverage, is a product of its times. The times accentuated a number of demographic and attitudinal trends that threatened to reduce levels of census cooperation with the census of 2000 and, in turn, to compromise levels of accuracy and coverage. Particularly worrisome was the differential undercount. A census that differentially enumerates across subgroups in the population is a census that falls short on the fairness criterion. The demographic and attitudinal challenges facing the Census Bureau in 2000 were different not in kind from those noted by George Washington in 1790, but in scope. It was this difference in scope that led the Census Bureau to explore aggressively the possibility of statistically adjusting the census results to reflect more accurately the demographic and geographical distribution of the American population.

The 2000 census also brought forth an unprecedented partisan fight over census methodology—the very methodology that, it was hoped, would "fix" the differential undercount even in the face of declining cooperation rates. As it turned out, statistical adjustment was not employed. The bureau encountered technical difficulties that were unresolved when the critical census products (for redistricting) had to be released. But the political maneuvering and the Supreme Court decision that preceded this outcome did result in a civic mobilization campaign unprecedented in its reach. How well did this campaign work? That is our initial empirical question.

Chapter Two | The Civic Mobilization Campaign

THE SOCIAL AND political environment facing the Census Bureau in 2000 posed a difficult challenge to completing a full and accurate count of the U.S. population. Population groups that are traditionally hard to locate and hard to count—immigrants, minorities, transients—were a growing proportion of the population as 2000 approached, and the public was generally less inclined toward civic participation. The bureau had experienced a disappointing cooperation rate a decade earlier, and the working assumption at the bureau, in Congress, and among knowledgeable observers was that the 2000 mail-back response would fall below the 1990 rate of 65 percent. It was also feared that the differential undercount would continue to worsen.

Although the Democratic White House and Republican Congress became embroiled in a heated controversy about sampling to correct for this undercount, the parties agreed that there should be a concerted and concentrated effort to enumerate undercounted groups using traditional methods. Toward that end, the 2000 census design included the most ambitious media and mobilization campaign ever undertaken, labeled by journalists as the "largest peacetime mobilization effort" in American history.

In this chapter, we evaluate that mobilization campaign, asking, simply, did it work? As discussed in the introduction, decades of research on campaign effects have provided reason to doubt that a media campaign could successfully mobilize census participation. Herman Hyman and Paul Sheatsley's (1947) early analysis, "Some Reasons Why Information Campaigns Fail," sums up the conventional wisdom in the public health field, and Thomas Holbrook's (1996) more recent work, *Do Campaigns Matter?*, offers the parallel perspective in political science. Information campaigns are thought to have little influence on public attitudes and behaviors because it is difficult to capture the attention of a busy public and

41

because, even if exposed, individuals have existing attitudes and predispositions that limit the persuasiveness of new information (Zaller 1992). Moreover, even if campaigns have a small or short-lived effect on the public, that influence is difficult to capture in observational evaluative studies (Iyengar 2001). Many scholars have concluded that campaigns are full of sound and fury, signifying nothing.

Whatever the academic standards for campaigns to "matter," the Census Bureau would have counted the campaign successful if it improved overall cooperation rates and/or if it differentially improved coverage among the traditionally undercounted groups. Either accomplishment would have been deemed cause for celebration; both would call for extra champagne. When the census was over, it seemed that, indeed, champagne was in order. Cooperation rates had improved more than expected, even exceeding 1990 levels, and the differential undercount had declined. But as the census ended, there was no way to know for certain that the mobilization campaign could be credited with these improvements. Only now, using a unique multimedia monitoring survey, can we confidently claim that the campaign was instrumental in the Census 2000 achievements. The information and mobilization efforts helped to reverse the decline in mail-back rates and, most notably, helped to increase cooperation among the hardest-to-count groups in the population.

CENSUS GOALS

Both of the Census Bureau's concerns leading up to 2000, the mail-back response rate and the differential undercount, are issues of census coverage—that is, determining how to enumerate as close to 100 percent of the population as possible. Based on the 1990 census response rate and recent social and demographic trends, the Census Bureau set a target mail-back response rate of 61 percent in 2000.[1] Although the 61 percent goal was below the already disappointing 1990 response rate, some believed even it to be an unrealistic goal. The General Accounting Office (GAO) warned Congress that the Census Bureau's mail response goal might be overly optimistic, and that if so, the bureau would face the problem of mounting a much larger field operation than planned in a difficult employment market and at much greater expense. Stephen Fienberg, former chair of the Committee on National Statistics, concluded that "all evidence suggests that a so-called traditional enumeration in 2000 will be demonstrably worse than in 1990, in terms of both omissions and erroneous enumerations" (U.S. Census Monitoring Board 1999, 5).[2]

Cost was one consideration behind the Census Bureau's goal of increasing mail-back cooperation. It is considerably more costly to enumerate a household via an in-person interview than by self-completed mail-back form. The GAO estimated that each percentage point of increased mail-back would save taxpayers $25 million. As shown in table 2.1, per household census costs had increased over the years as mail-back response rates declined. The cost per household increased from just $13 in 1970 to $32 in 1990.

Poor response rates not only are costly but also contribute to deterioration in data quality. Forms completed closer to Census Day (April 1, 2000) were subject to fewer errors of recall than those completed months later when the follow-up phase of the census was finishing the last cases. And during follow-up the shift to interviewer-completed forms introduced additional sources of error—misunderstandings between the interviewer and respondent and a respondent's eagerness to please can lead to flawed data.[3] Beyond these cost and quality concerns, the mail-back response rate would indicate whether the government could rely on the civic responsibility and legal compliance of the populace to conduct one of its most basic duties—its decadal constitutional obligation to apportion political power according to population distribution.

Although the mail-back response rate is an indicator of how well the census is working across the entire population, the related issue of public cooperation focuses on population groups known to be hard to count, that is, the troubling *differential undercount.* The census has always undercounted the population, but some Americans, especially minorities, are missed more often than others. With the 1990 census, the Census Bureau estimated that it missed less than 1 percent (.007 percent) of the non-Hispanic white population, but at least 12 percent of Native Americans living on reservations, 5 percent of Hispanics, and 4.4 percent of African Americans.

The differential undercount draws attention to an important distinction in statistical accuracy—the distinction between the *numerical* and *distributional* accuracy of a census count. Numerical accuracy is the extent to which the final count approximates the true number of residents on Census Day. Distributional accuracy is the extent to which the census count reflects the

Table 2.1   Cost of the U.S. Census, 1970 to 1990

Census Year	Cost per Household (Constant U.S. Dollars)
1970	$13
1980	24
1990	32

Source: General Accounting Office (2001b).

true proportional geographic or demographic distribution of the population. Distributional inaccuracy begins to matter when benefits from a fixed resource are allocated proportionate to population shares—as, of course, in the apportionment of congressional seats and votes in the Electoral College.

A census can be distributionally accurate even if numerically inaccurate. For example, if the census misses the same percentage of the population in every state, then each state receives the same number of congressional seats it would have even if 100 percent of the population had been counted. It is when the percentage of census omissions differs from one state to the next that there is distributional inaccuracy. The same logic holds for the demographically based concept of the differential undercount. Racial minorities would not be penalized if their undercount rate matched that of the population at large. But this is not what happens. Moreover, the differential undercount can persist even if the census is very successful in reaching the vast majority of the population.

Consider the following hypothetical census: assume that, out of 120 million households, 90 million mail back a census form, leaving 30 million to be visited by enumerators, of which 28 million cooperate, leaving 2 million households not in the census, of which 1.5 million are racial minorities. In this illustration, only a small percentage (1.67 percent) of the households are missed, but those missed are disproportionately concentrated among minorities (75 percent). Given that census numbers are used to distribute power and money, it is readily apparent that the differential undercount touches issues of social justice, voting rights, and equality. On the eve of the 2000 census, as Congress was debating the use of statistical corrections, the differential undercount became the focus of civil rights leaders. Rev. Jesse Jackson urged African Americans to "stand up and be counted or be counted out!" (*Ebony* 2000). Marvin Raines, associate director for field operations for the Census Bureau, called taking part in the census "a matter of pride. There's the whole issue of respect. When you have the numbers, people listen. There's something to be said about the adage that 'there is strength in numbers' " (*Ebony* 2000). At an African American leadership summit dedicated to the 2000 census, Dr. Joseph Lowery, chair of the Black Leadership Forum, gave the charge, "*You* must bell the cat. We are they whom God is calling today to get out yonder into our neighborhoods and our ghettoes and get our folk counted. Let's get our people counted and make our future count" (National Coalition on Black Civic Participation 1999).

The differential undercount is a difficult problem, and along with the mail-back rate, it became a preoccupation as the Census Bureau designed its effort to improve public cooperation. Improving the mail-back response rate and reducing the differential undercount are, of course, related efforts.

Returning to our hypothetical census, assume that the census mail-back rate is not 60 percent, or even 75 percent, but 90 percent or better. In this (very unlikely) scenario, the Census Bureau would focus all of its field resources on the comparatively smaller number of remaining households and be able to bring the differential undercount to a negligible level.

No one expected such a census, so a campaign to improve public cooperation was designed around the two goals of urging the public to mail back the census form and targeting special efforts in the hard-to-count population groups. With these goals at the forefront in 2000, an already expensive undertaking became more so. Budgeting for the census in 2000, however, benefited from the heady economy of the late 1990s. Tax revenues were sharply up, and in this fiscally comfortable environment, the Republican-led Congress willingly paid for a more expensive census. There were political calculations involved as well. Having successfully challenged the less costly plan designed to reduce the undercount using statistical methods, Republicans were attacked by Democrats as not wanting a census that would be fair to minorities. The strongest retort available to the Republicans was generous funding, in particular those dollars targeted to reducing the undercount of racial minorities: the extra funds for community partnerships and promotional campaigns, the higher salaries for enumerators working in difficult-to-count areas, and additional financial support for outreach programs in remote areas and places with high immigrant concentrations.

Ironically, though the earliest planning for the census was guided by firm congressional direction to hold costs down, Congress eventually funded the 2000 census at nearly twice the level of the previous one; one result was a very ambitious public outreach effort.

THE PUBLIC OUTREACH EFFORT

We focus here on the advertising campaign and the partnership program, but we should mention that the Census Bureau undertook a number of other efforts to reduce the hurdles to the public's cooperation with the census. Lack of language skills, for example, is one of the barriers to any form of civic participation, including sending in a census form. To lower this barrier, census questionnaires were printed in five languages commonly used in the United States in addition to English, and both telephone assistance center staff and enumerator staff were multilingual. The multiple ways for the public to respond—by mail, by phone, by Internet, or by going to a walk-in assistance center—were all multilingual as well. In addition, the call centers could conduct phone interviews with individuals who had literacy problems, those who had physical or other handicaps, or those others who operators determined could not otherwise fill out the form. Those who felt that they had been missed could pick up a "Be Counted" form at a community center or other convenient location; thus, anyone motivated to participate could do so even without receiving a census form. Providing multiple ways to respond ran the risk of including some people twice, however, and in fact that became a problem in the 2000 census.[4]

The information campaign included three direct mailings: an advance notice to every household saying that the census form would be arriving, the census form itself, and then a postcard thanking respondents for returning the form or reminding them to do so. These mailings not only helped to keep the census salient but also gave some prominence to the legal obligation to return the census form—a potentially effective, if stark, incentive. On the envelope was stamped the message "Your Response Is Required by Law: U.S. Census Form Enclosed." Thus, for the first time the Census Bureau used the questionnaire itself as a channel of communication.

The paid-advertising campaign and partnership activities downplayed the legal obligation and instead emphasized "fair share." This message tracks back to the $200 billion in federal funds distributed each year in part through formulas that take population size as well as population and housing characteristics into account. Because census data have a ten-year life, $2 trillion, in principle, is at stake. The bureau's campaign relentlessly stressed that cooperation would shape the future of one's community in ways beneficial to family, friends, and neighbors. The two most prominent aspects of the census campaign efforts were paid media advertising and census community partnerships.

Paid Advertising

The first task of the Census Bureau was to ensure awareness of the census; the second was to motivate cooperation. Toward those goals, the bureau mounted an extensive (and expensive), targeted, paid-advertising campaign. In contrast, previous censuses had relied exclusively on free public service ads. Such ads made generic appeals ("The government needs this information; please cooperate") rather than targeting specific groups, and they were careful to avoid making a hard sell or having too much of an edge. As public service ads, they typically ran late at night or on programs with small audiences. Large-audience programs were too valuable as sources of paid-advertising revenue for networks to place public service announcements during them.

In contrast, and for the first time in history, the census in 2000 paid market rates, and a $165 million budget was large enough to enable the bureau to compete in any outlet at any time of day. Even the most expensive ad buys were not out of reach, as illustrated by the well-received Super Bowl ad. The census budget was second in size only to McDonald's and Wendy's during the early months of 2000.

The ad messages also received a major overhaul. A major Madison Avenue agency, Young and Rubicam, designed the campaign, working closely with specialty firms experienced in reaching African Americans, Hispanics, Asians, American Indians, and immigrant groups. These firms designed highly targeted ads and took care to place them in outlets that would reach their intended audience. Every possible outlet—TV, radio, newspapers, magazines, billboards, and posters in buses and commercial outlets—was used to place 253 different ads, appearing in seven languages. The campaign reached 99 percent of the adult population.

Every ad included a facsimile of the census form itself, along with the tag line: "This is your future, don't leave it blank." Ads emphasized that cooperating with the census would benefit one's community in tangible ways—less crowded schools, more public transportation, better emergency service. The not-so-subtle message was that an uncooperative community would get less than its share of publicly funded benefits. This message was well illustrated in one poster that in the end was not used because it had perhaps too much of an edge. It showed a tax form and a census form side by side, with the tag line: "This form taketh away. This form giveth back."

The paid-advertising campaign started in late 1999 with messages designed to increase awareness across the entire population and was followed by a much more targeted campaign that peaked in the mail-back period of the census operation, approximately mid-March to mid-April 2000. The advertising then shifted in emphasis during the follow-up phase of census-taking, stressing the importance of cooperating when census enumerators visited those households that had failed to return a form by mail. Because our focus is on the mail-back response rate, however, we investigate in this chapter the impact of the ad campaign during the period from early March to mid-April.[5]

Partnerships

Not confident that paid advertising would be adequate to arrest the decline in census cooperation, the Census Bureau established an unprecedented number of partnerships with state and local governments, community groups, and businesses—140,000 in all. A special subset of these, Complete Count Committees, involved state, county, and city government officials in promoting the census. The twelve thousand Complete Count Committees sponsored promotional events, worked with local media to publicize census activities, and helped the Census Bureau in key areas such as recruiting temporary staff and providing enumerator training facilities. The Census Bureau would eventually hire and train nearly one million temporary employees at a time when the unemployment rate was at historic lows. Notably, the Complete Count Committees self-funded most of the activities they sponsored. In addition, sixty thousand volunteers staffed community sites in churches, schools, clubhouses, and similar meeting places where "Be Counted" forms were available. A school program placed census-related curricular material in thousands of classrooms. Census vans, first seen on NBC's *Today Show,* toured the country visiting fairs, sporting events, hard-to-count neighborhoods, and other places with the aim of being covered by the local media.

Hundreds of special events and promotions were held across the nation. The Census Bureau did not keep a count of the number of invitations extended to the director to participate in these events, but he did keep track of how many he attended—more than one hundred from mid-January through April. His favorite was the first-person-to-be-counted event in Unalakleet, Alaska (see photo 2.1).

In addition to the Census Bureau's own partnership budget of $143 million, promotional dollars were contributed by hundreds of local and state governments and by private businesses and other groups. California alone had a state budget of $35 million to promote Census 2000. State and local governments were motivated to participate by self-interest—accurate counts of their cities and towns would directly influence the amount of federal monies they received. One study estimates that a single uncounted individual costs a community $5,300 in federal monies over a ten-year period (Vigdor 2001, 6). Local newspaper stories, for example, repeatedly stressed how much their community had "lost" by not being fully counted in the 1990 census. The Census Bureau estimated that New York City alone lost more than $415 million in federal funds during the 1990s owing to the undercount.

Although some of these 140,000 partnerships were in name only, a post-census survey of partnership activities reports that approximately 100,000 of them sponsored separate promotional and motivational events (Wolter et al. 2002, 28, R111). The following examples offer just a few illustrations of the wide range of activities organized through the partnership program.

- McDonald's in Detroit rewarded homeless people who completed a form with a free meal and a yellow button saying, "I'm Important, I've Been Counted."

- Radio Fiesta, a network of twenty south Florida stations, aired a special series of announcements that reached 100,000 migrant and seasonal workers.

Photo 2.1   Census Director Kenneth Prewitt in Unalakleet, Alaska, on His Way to Count the First Person in Census 2000

Source: Reproduced with permission from AP/Wide World Photos.

- The Carolina Panthers of the National Football League gave free exhibition space at home games, allowing census workers to reach tens of thousands of football fans throughout North and South Carolina.

- Milwaukee spent $350,000 on its "I Will Count in Census 2000" campaign, one of hundreds of instances of state and local governments spending their own funds on census promotion.

- Univision, the Spanish-language TV channel, covered the census heavily, including a national broadcast of a census-focused Mass from the San Antonio Cathedral, the oldest in the nation, that reached millions of listeners.

- The Navajo Nation hosted a tribal leadership conference to promote census cooperation and help recruit Navajo-speaking enumerators.

- Churches promoted the census, distributing material and cooperating with a "census Sabbath" program. The Catholic Church was especially active in reaching out to recent Mexican and Central American immigrants, stressing that census answers were confidential.

One particularly notable partnership effort was the "1990 Plus 5 percent" campaign (fondly called the "get it up" campaign by some census staffers)— the challenge to every city, county, and state in the nation to improve its 1990 census response rate by five percentage points. This ambitious campaign, which declared that the nation should not only stop the declining cooperation rate but actually reverse it, was not part of the initial mobilization design but emerged as an afterthought of a speech given by the bureau director in New Orleans. Back at census headquarters, the thought was greeted, understandably, with resistance and skepticism—resistance because it is not a good idea to introduce untested procedures into an ongoing operation as complicated as a census, and certainly not a procedure that might deflect staff attention away from assigned tasks; and skepticism because the best models available did not justify expecting the response rate to be above 61 percent, the figure on which the census had been budgeted and staffed. With some anxious moments, the director persisted, and eventually the bureau figured out how to report every day to 39,000 jurisdictions in the country—villages, towns, cities, Indian reservations, counties—their mailback "score." These day-by-day scores were widely cited in the press; *USA Today* reported not only the national totals but the response rate for each of the fifty states. Cities competed with each other, and at least one case of wine passed from a mayor to his counterpart in a neighboring town whose rate came in higher. Knowledgeable census watchers, including the associate director with day-to-day line management responsibilities for the census, credited the "Plus 5" campaign with helping a number of towns and cities improve their mail-back rates by as much as the 5 percent target.

Of course, it is not easy to separate out the effect of different components of the mobilization campaign, though anecdotal data, personal experience with the census, and our data analysis suggest that the paid advertising had greater reach than other aspects of the campaign. But the data also indicate that programs such as the "Plus 5" campaign, the census-in-the-schools effort, the outreach of the Catholic Church, and the urban focus of the Complete Count Committees were especially effective in improving cooperation by the traditionally hard-to-count population groups. The habitually cautious General Accounting Office (2001a, 9), which audited the census partnership program, concluded that "it appears as though key census-taking activities, such as encouraging people to return their questionnaires, would have been less successful had it not been for the Census Bureau's partnership efforts."

We offer an empirical assessment of the effectiveness of the census campaign efforts. As we discussed in the introduction, much of the academic research on campaign effects has focused on methods for evaluating the impact of the campaign. Our approach is to measure the campaign in as many different ways as possible and to evaluate the influence of the campaign on census awareness, knowledge, attitudes, and behavior, taking into account that information campaigns can influence the public both through persuasion and learning (Yanovitzky and Stryker 2001).

CENSUS AWARENESS

The initial challenge of an information campaign is simply to increase public awareness. Certainly this is so for the census; if Americans are aware of the census at all, they typically think of it as a dull counting project carried out by the government from time to time. Ask why a census is taken, and Americans vaguely reply that the government seems to need all these numbers; if pressed, a very few might be able to recall that the census has something to do with congressional reapportioning or with how federal monies are spent.

From the perspective even of those who are aware of the decennial count, the census is an infrequent and low-salience event. Generally only one person in the household sees the census form, and if this is the short form (sent to 83 percent of households), it takes on average just three minutes to complete. (Even the long form takes only thirty-eight minutes on average.) Something that takes three (or even thirty-eight) minutes every ten years is, in terms of visibility, hardly comparable to most civic or political acts—especially those accompanying a presidential campaign with its wall-to-wall media coverage stretching across many months every four years. A 1999 study that found that fewer than half of adult Americans knew the census was going to take place in the next year concluded: "Our national survey of Americans' attitudes toward the Census sends the message that Census 2000 has yet to be introduced to the public, and the Census Bureau has a considerable task ahead to grab the country's attention. Most Americans are unaware that the Census will take place next year or that the country takes a census every 10 years" (Belden Russonello and Stewart Research and Communications, 1999, 4).

In assessing the effectiveness of the census campaign, we must first determine whether the information provided to the public helped to increase its awareness of the decennial census. Did the census campaign catch the attention of a busy public distracted by the information overload of a saturated media environment in which the only defense is channel surfing, web browsing, and other forms of selective media consumption? We address this question using the Stanford Institute for the Quantitative Study of Society monitoring surveys. From early March 2000 through mid-April 2000, a series of five nationally representative surveys asked, "How much have you seen or heard about the census from (TV commercials or public service announcements/radio advertisements/newspaper advertisements)?" with the possible responses "a lot," "a little," or "not at all."

Figure 2.1 reports the percentage of respondents who saw, heard, or read census-related advertising over the course of the final weeks of the census campaign. Awareness increased at least 20 to 30 percent for each media outlet, with TV exposure reaching 95 percent, followed by radio (77 percent) and print (71 percent). These sharp increases actually underestimate the impact of the media campaign, since the advertising had been under way for more than two months by the time of our first survey. What figure 2.1 does confirm is that by the end of the mail-back phase of the census, practically no one was unaware that a census was under way. As Young and Rubicam's executive vice president responsible for the advertising contract commented, it was clear that the campaign had been successful when the census became "part of the popular buzz." She had in mind, for example, that Jay Leno and David Letterman had made the census a joke target, and that it was the subject of a comedy sketch on *Saturday Night Live* (McCarty 2004).

The mobilization appeals through community organizations, including churches and schools, required a different type of coordination than that for the media advertising. As noted, thousands of local governments, churches, businesses, schools, and community organizations joined in the promotion effort. These community-based appeals reached fewer people

Figure 2.1   Exposure to Census Campaign Over Time, by Media Type

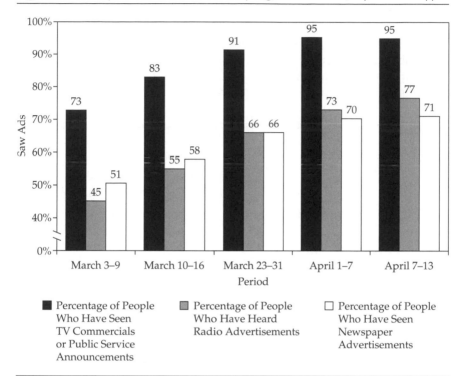

Source: Authors' compilation, SIQSS census monitors, 2000.
Note: The change between the first and final observation periods is statistically significant at p < .001 for all three items.

than paid advertising, but the numbers were nevertheless substantial. By mid-April, half of the American population had heard about the census from at least one community group, speeches by government officials had reached more than one-quarter of the population, and more than one-sixth had heard about the census from a government organization. Nearly two million educators in public, private, tribal, and parochial schools had received "Making Sense of Census 2000" by the time Census 2000 questionnaires reached most households. We find that 8 percent of respondents reported hearing about the census through school-related activities, and 9 percent learned about the census from materials that children brought home from school. About 6 percent heard about the census from meetings of a religious group.

Although the community-based efforts and the outreach through the partnership program were largely voluntary—and thus emerged wherever local leaders were engaged enough to create events or activities—the Census Bureau's own partnership staff, which it hired and trained, was focused on reaching the traditionally undercounted groups: racial minorities, immigrants (including illegal immigrants), and other hard-to-count groups. Our data allow us to detect whether the community-based effort was disproportionately successful in reaching racial/ethnic minorities. In figure 2.2, we use the final monitoring survey to show the percentage of African Americans, Hispanics, and whites who reported having heard from each of the community organizations. We find that a far greater proportion of African Americans and Hispanics heard about the census from their church, from local community and government organizations, and from school-related activities and census material brought home by children.

We illustrate the over-time pattern of contact from community groups in figure 2.3, which shows that African American respondents were consistently exposed to community groups at roughly twice the rate of the white respondents. (By early April, blacks had heard from an average of about 1.4 groups, while whites had heard from fewer than 0.6 groups.)

Figure 2.2   Heard About Census from Community Groups, by Minority Status

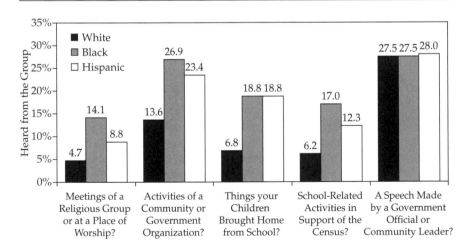

Have You Seen or Heard Anything About the Census from...

Source: Authors' compilation, SIQSS census fifth monitor, April 7–13, 2000.

Figure 2.3   Average Number of Groups That Respondent Heard from
About Census, by Racial Groups

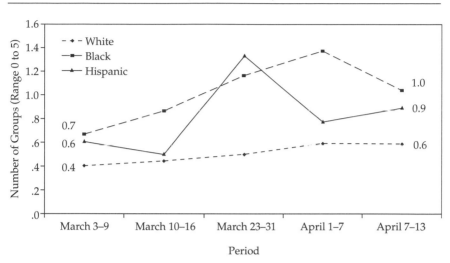

Source: Authors' compilation, SIQSS census monitors, 2000.
Note: N = 3252 (whites); 451 (blacks), 337 (Hispanics).

By the end of the campaign, two-thirds of the black population had heard from at least one community group, compared to just half of the white population. Exposure differences are particularly pronounced in church-based census exposure: three times the proportion of blacks (16 percent) heard about the census in church at some point during the campaign, compared to just 5 percent of whites.[6] Similar, though less dramatic, patterns are true of the Hispanic population, which was generally more exposed to the campaign than whites but somewhat less exposed than blacks.

The self-reported exposure measures used thus far suggest that the census campaign was successful at reaching target population groups, but self-reported measures inevitably contain considerable error.[7] People have trouble recalling the details of a low-salience event like a single radio or TV ad. Thus, responses to a "how much" question no doubt rely on a considerable amount of guesswork. Likewise, individuals may have different definitions of how much "a lot" or "a little" exposure is. Finally, a vague recollection of seeing an advertisement at some point is not the same as paying enough attention to the advertisement to comprehend and later remember the message.

We have taken advantage of the multimedia capabilities of Knowledge Networks to create a more reliable measure of exposure to television advertising. Respondents in each of the monitoring surveys were asked about their recognition of *particular* ads, as shown to them with a still screen shot from a television ad. The advertising frames, shown in figure 2.4, are taken from the four most widely played ads, labeled "Crowded Schools," "Day Care," "Emergency Services," and "Icon." The first ad shows a door, marked CUSTODIAL SUPPLIES, in a school hall; when the door opens as a class bell rings, it becomes clear that the janitor's closet is being used as a classroom. The "Day Care" ad has a similar message, showing a young waitress in danger of losing her job because she has again brought her child to work. A couple in "Emergency Services" watch a fire raging through their barn and worry about whether the fire department has arrived in time to save it. Finally,

Figure 2.4   Census Television Ads, 2000

Crowded Schools

Day Care

Emergency Services

Icon

Source: U.S. Census Bureau, 2000.

"Icon" offers an iconographic presentation of familiar, impressive scenes in Washington, D.C. The uniform message of these advertisements is that various government services and benefits are distributed on the basis of the size and characteristics of the population and that cooperating with the census will bring more of those benefits to each community.

Using this recognition measure of advertising exposure to illustrate over-time exposure to the census campaign, we find a similar trend. Figure 2.5 shows a steady increase in the percentage of respondents recognizing at least one ad as the campaign unfolded.

Particularly impressive are the ad recognition levels by race, shown in figure 2.6. Recognition of specific advertising frames increased for all racial groups, but more sharply for the targeted groups. By mid-April, the proportion of blacks recognizing at least one advertising frame had increased to nearly 90 percent from a base of 55 percent in early March. Hispanics had a similar 35 percent increase in recognition. The change in advertising recognition by the white population, though substantial, was less dramatic, with a 27-percentage-point increase.

Figure 2.5   Recognized at Least One Census TV Ad Frame

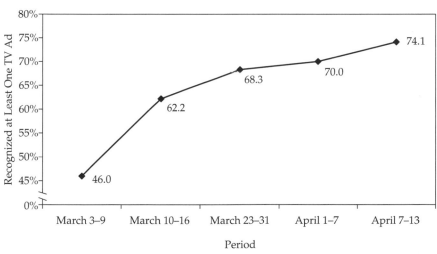

Source: Authors' compilation, SIQSS census monitors, 2000.
Notes: N = 992 (March 3–9); 972 (March 10–16); 652 (March 23–31); 947 (April 1–7); 894 (April 7–13). The change from March 3–9 to April 7–13 is significant at the level of p < .001. Ads taken into account: "Day Care," "Icon," "Emergency Services," "Crowded Schools."

Figure 2.6   Recognized at Least One TV Ad Frame, by Race

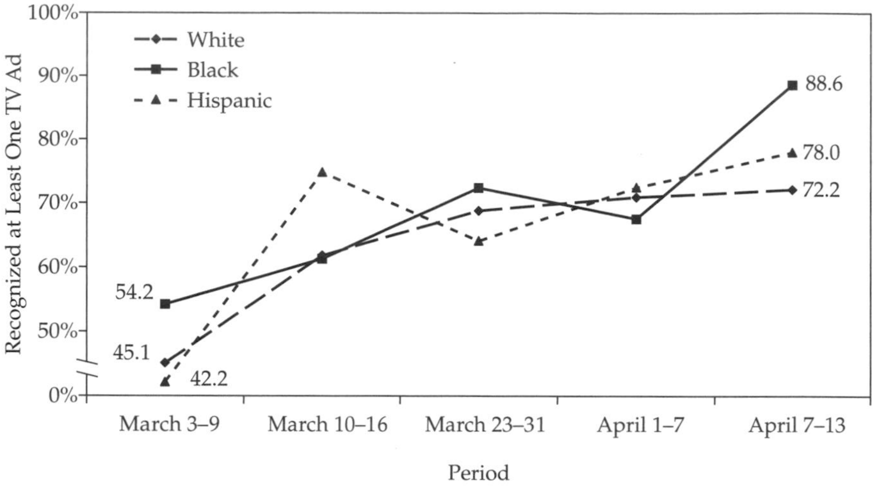

Source: Authors' compilation, SIQSS census monitors, 2000.
Notes: N = 3252 (whites); 451 (blacks); 337 (Hispanics). Ads counted: "Day Care," "Icon," "Emergency Services," "Crowded Schools."

To further test whether the ads had their intended effect and to evaluate which ads were most persuasive, we again capitalized on the technological capabilities of our web-based survey methodology. Respondents were shown a video of a complete census ad. After viewing the video, respondents were asked whether the ad captured their attention, was specifically talking to them, and would make them want to participate in the census. This method combines the advantages of a focus group with a nationally representative sample. It offers a considerable advantage over standard designs using video footage, which typically limit their samples to a local community (or college undergraduates) and rely on unnatural settings such as a college classroom for the video viewing. In our study, which used a nationally representative sample of respondents, video viewing occurred in the individual's own home, at his or her convenience.

The ads shown included the four just discussed (all of which were designed for a general audience) as well as three others that were more specifically targeted to minority groups. "Talking Census" includes animation in which the census form asks that it not be discarded. The other two, "Anthem" and "Tribute," feature black and Hispanic children. These three ads were targeted to TV programs with large minority audiences.[8]

In analyzing reactions to the videos, we find that 62 percent of respondents said that the ads they had just seen captured their attention (ranging from 50 percent for "Icon" to 67 percent for "Talking Census"). Forty-three percent said that seeing the ad made them want to participate in the census, with "Icon" scoring lowest (34 percent) and "Crowded Schools" scoring highest (50 percent). Because three of the ads were in fact intended to reach different audiences, we are most interested in a comparison of respondent reactions to the advertisements by race, reported in table 2.2. The pattern is clear: racial differences are much stronger, always reaching statistical significance, for the three ads designed for minority audiences.

Table 2.2   Reactions to TV Ads, by Race, 2000

	Percentage Agree (Count)			Chi-square
	Whites	Blacks	Hispanics	p-value
Did the ad capture your attention?				
"Day Care"	65 (404)	67 (52)	64 (50)	.90
"Icon"	47 (453)	63 (65)	59 (59)	.10
"Emergency Services"	64 (413)	63 (54)	68 (41)	.70
"Crowded Schools"	63 (410)	65 (43)	70 (54)	.60
"Talking Census"	62 (369)	76 (62)	92 (39)	.005
"Anthem"	51 (419)	81 (47)	81 (37)	.001
"Tribute"	48 (438)	78 (54)	68 (47)	.001
Was the ad talking to you?				
"Day Care"	18 (368)	9 (44)	25 (48)	.40
"Icon"	29 (420)	40 (60)	31 (55)	.05
"Emergency Services"	22 (372)	26 (51)	22 (36)	.60
"Crowded Schools"	24 (362)	32 (37)	46 (44)	.05
"Talking Census"	19 (335)	39 (57)	32 (34)	.01
"Anthem"	19 (385)	47 (45)	51 (35)	.001
"Tribute"	16 (399)	51 (49)	49 (43)	.001
Did the ad make you want to participate in the census?				
"Day Care"	43 (385)	56 (27)	48 (24)	.05
"Icon"	32 (424)	47 (58)	38 (60)	.10
"Emergency Services"	44 (383)	50 (52)	50 (36)	.90
"Crowded Schools"	46 (372)	71 (48)	70 (50)	.01
"Talking Census"	38 (345)	55 (66)	67 (36)	.001
"Anthem"	32 (398)	52 (44)	71 (38)	.001
"Tribute"	32 (407)	61 (51)	57 (42)	.001

Source: Authors' compilation, SIQSS census monitors, 2000.

To summarize the analysis thus far, we offer two general conclusions regarding exposure to the census campaign. First, different components of the mobilization campaign—paid advertising and promotion through community partnerships—all helped to bring the census to public awareness. What the public came to believe about the census and the effect on behavior remain to be analyzed, but by any reasonable standard the mobilization campaign achieved its initial goal—drawing the attention of the American public to the once-a-decade census. Second, the Census Bureau was successful in meeting its goal of reaching the hardest-to-count groups in the population.

So far so good, but the test that matters is not awareness but cooperation. As we discussed in the introduction, it is easier to bring attention to an issue than to influence attitudes (or behavior) on that issue. For instance, public health communication campaigns have been found to increase public awareness of health risks, but behavior change in response to campaign messages is rarely found (see, for example, Atkin and Wallack 1990). Did the census advertising campaign help to improve cooperation rates and reduce the differential undercount?

KNOWLEDGE OF AND OPINIONS ABOUT THE CENSUS

If the campaign messages were effective beyond simply increasing awareness, we would expect the public to become more knowledgeable about the census and to view it more favorably. At aggregate levels, it is evident that the mobilization effort led to higher levels of census knowledge. Figure 2.7 indicates that factual knowledge about the census grew as the mobilization campaign progressed. According to our monitoring surveys, the proportion of the population that correctly identified the census as being held every ten years (as opposed to some other interval) grew from about 60 percent in early March to almost 80 percent by early April. This level of knowledge was maintained at this heightened level through mid-April, when all the forms were supposed to have been mailed back to the Census Bureau. As with other measures, our survey results cannot pick up the pre-March effects of promotion and advertising that started several weeks earlier.

Similarly, we find that less than 20 percent of the public knew in early March that filling out the census form was mandated by law. By the end of March, when all the census forms had been mailed out, the proportion had more than doubled, with nearly 50 percent understanding their legal obligation. This change is no doubt related to a number of aspects of the information campaign, especially the census mailings and news coverage. The three mailings used by the Census Bureau itself, especially the

Figure 2.7   Learning During the Census Campaign of 2000

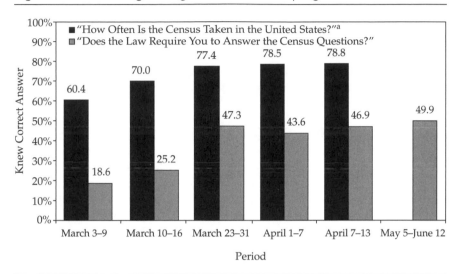

Source: Authors' compilation, SIQSS census monitors and a follow-up, 2000.

Notes: N = 992 (March 3–9); 968 (March 10–16); 652 (March 23–31); 945 (April 1–7); 894 (April 7–13); 2,397 (May 5–June 12). The change between the first and last observation periods is statistically significant at p < .001 for both items.
[a] "How often is the census taken in the United States?" was not measured in May 5–June 12.

advance letter and the census form, stressed the legal obligation to return the form. Indeed, there was a particularly sharp increase in census knowledge in the last two weeks of March when the census form reached 120 million households.

Looking at knowledge dynamics by race, we find increases in knowledge about the census across minority groups. Figure 2.8 indicates that blacks and Hispanics remained, on average, slightly less knowledgeable than whites by Census Day, but all racial groups exhibited impressive gains in census knowledge between early March and mid-April.

Notably, we find no change in general political knowledge over this same time period. This offers additional evidence that the change in census knowledge is attributable to the census campaign rather than something else—say, greater attention to the news because of the impending presidential campaign.

Attitudes about the census, in contrast, did not change nearly as much during this period. To determine whether the mobilization message, focusing on the community benefits, resonated with the public, we use two agree/

Figure 2.8   Census Knowledge over Time for Racial Groups

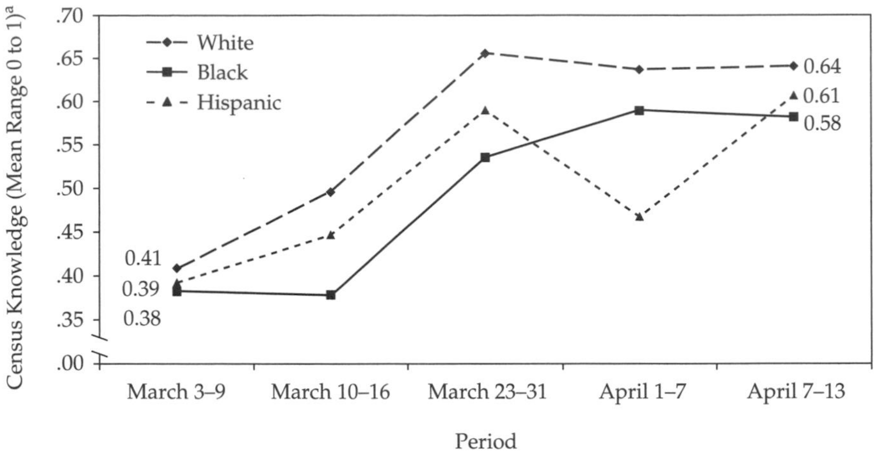

Source: Authors' compilation, SIQSS census monitors, 2000.
Notes: The increase in knowledge from March 3–9 to April 7–13 is significant (p < .001) for all racial groups. N = 3,246 (whites); 451 (blacks); 335 (Hispanics).
[a]Census knowledge is average score on two items: (1) "How often is the census taken in the United States?" and (2) "Does the law require you to answer the census questions?"

disagree statements: "The census will let the government know what people in the community need," and "It matters that I personally fill out the census form."

We find that there were high levels of agreement on these items by the time we started our data series (about 72 percent on both items), and that the level of agreement stayed high throughout the observation period (in the range of 72 to 75 percent). This suggests that the general advertising campaign starting several weeks earlier had already established this high base agreement or that it tapped into prior prevailing beliefs about the census. Because the agreement level was high already by early March, it is not possible to trace opinion change to the campaign with our data.[9] One suggestive bit of evidence, however, is that a separate national survey in 1999 commissioned by the U.S. Census Monitoring Board found substantially fewer positive opinions about the census (Belden Russonello and Stewart Research and Communications 1999).[10] The 1999 survey found that just over five in ten Americans strongly agreed that "it is important for me to participate in the Census because the Census count helps to determine the amount of government funds my community receives" (54 percent), that "the Census is a way for me and people like me to be counted in society" (53 percent), and that "the Census is important to give me and my community political representation and power" (52 percent) (Belden Russonello and Stewart Research and Communications 1999, 8). And nearly half (48 percent) of the public identified with the statement: "My personal participation in the Census does not really matter that much in a population of over 250 million people" (10). This suggests that the campaign probably led to more positive attitudes toward the census, but our monitoring surveys were not in the field early enough to capture the movement. In the next chapter, we explore how negative attitudes toward the census, anchored in a debate over privacy, did change in observable ways over the course of the census.

CENSUS COOPERATION

On two dimensions—awareness of and knowledge about the census—the mobilization campaign appeared to be successful, but did the campaign influence behavior? Since that is the issue that matters, here we ask whether the campaign helped to improve census cooperation across the general population, and then particularly among the hard-to-count groups on which so much of the campaign was focused.

We start by evaluating whether exposure to the census campaign was related to census cooperation. Figure 2.9 reports the average number of ads recognized by individuals who reported returning their census compared to those who did not. We see that, on average, respondents who returned their census form recognized more census ads than those who did not. It indeed appears that increased exposure to the census campaign was associated with mail-back cooperation. Because we are interested not only in general levels of cooperation but in the consequences of the campaign for the differential undercount, we look at race differences in cooperation and exposure. The pattern is strong, as shown in figure 2.10. Whereas the average number of ads recognized by whites differs little between those who returned their census forms and those who did not (1.15 ads versus 1.27 ads), the differences between blacks and Hispanics is dramatic. For African Americans, the average number of ads recognized for those who returned their census form exceeds that of whites (1.41 ads) and is roughly double that of blacks who did not return their census form (0.72 ads). Likewise, Hispanics who returned their census form also recognized, on average, more census ads than whites who returned their census form (1.41), and significantly more than Hispanics who did not return their census form (0.88). This initial cut of the data suggests that census cooperation was related to exposure to the advertising campaign, especially among the minority groups targeted by the campaign.

Figure 2.9   Number of Census TV Ad Frames Recognized,
              by Census Mail-Back

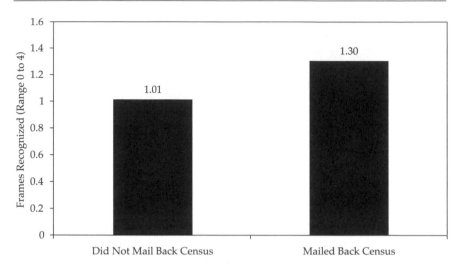

Source: Authors' compilation, SIQSS census monitors and a follow-up, 2000.

Although this analysis is very encouraging, we want to model directly the effect of the census campaign on census cooperation while taking into account other factors that can influence mail-back rates. We therefore estimate a multivariate logistic regression model to predict the effect of census exposure on individual-level mail-back cooperation, controlling for marital status, education, race, gender, age, work status, and urban/rural status. We measure census exposure in two ways. First, we measure it directly by the number of census advertisements recognized (ranging from zero to four advertisements).[11] To link the campaign more clearly to census participation, we also take advantage of the before-and-after panel component of the SIQSS surveys and measure *individual-level changes* in census knowledge. Thus, we can assess whether there was a learning effect from the campaign that might be related to census cooperation above and beyond an individual's baseline census knowledge.[12]

Table 2.3 reports the key results from this multivariate model. (The full set of coefficients, standard errors, and model fit statistics are included in table 2A.1.) The results in table 2.3 show that, even controlling for demographic predictors, campaign exposure was related to a higher likelihood of returning the census form. The positive and statistically significant

Figure 2.10   Census TV Ad Frames Recognized, by Census Mail-Back and Race

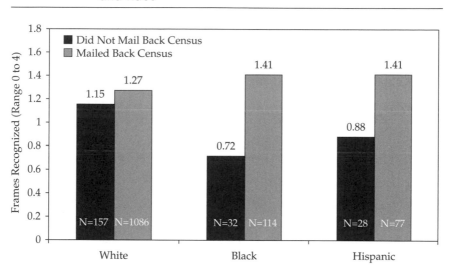

Source: Authors' compilation, SIQSS census monitors and a follow-up, 2000.

advertising exposure coefficient indicates that an increase in the number of census ads recognized increases the likelihood that an individual would return a census form. The substantive interpretation of this coefficient can be seen in figure 2.11.[13] Holding all else constant, individuals who recognized no census ads had a 54 percent predicted likelihood of returning their census form. In contrast, individuals who recognized all four census ads had a 73 percent likelihood of returning their census form. So our model predicts that census advertising can increase the

Table 2.3   Census Campaign Exposure Effects from the Multivariate Model

Campaign Exposure and Knowledge	Coefficients
Number of ads recognized	.217**
Census knowledge (baseline)	1.813***
Change in census knowledge	1.464***

Source: Authors' compilation, SIQSS census monitors and follow-up, 2000, short form only.
Notes: For full results, see model 1 in table 2A.1. Valid N = 1,274.
**p < .01; ***p < .001

Figure 2.11   Predicted Probability of Census Mail-Back Cooperation, by Number of TV Ads Recognized

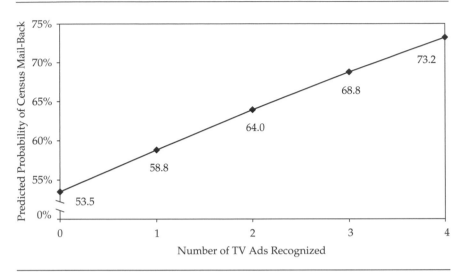

Source: Authors' compilation, SIQSS census monitors and a follow-up, 2000.

probability of mail-back cooperation by as much as twenty percentage points.

Turning to our second measure of census exposure, we find that individuals who learned about the census over the course of the campaign were more likely to mail back their census form, even controlling for baseline levels of census knowledge and demographics. The positive and statistically significant coefficient for census knowledge indicates that those who already knew the census is required by law were more likely to return their census; the positive and statistically significant coefficient for change in census knowledge indicates that those who learned over the course of the campaign that the census is required by law were also significantly more likely to return their census form. The substantive impact of this learning effect is quite large. Using these coefficients to calculate the predicted probability of mail-back cooperation, we find that learning the legal requirement over the course of the campaign increased the predicted likelihood of mail-back cooperation from 53 to 83 percent. Combining the direct advertising exposure effect and the indirect learning effect, we find that the census campaign had a sizable impact on census cooperation. To illustrate the potential total effect of the census campaign, we graph in figure 2.12 the predicted levels of census mail-back cooperation at each level

Figure 2.12   Predicted Census Mail-Back Cooperation,
                by Campaign Efforts

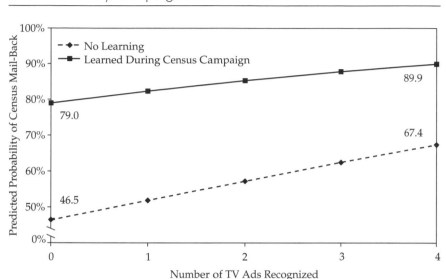

Source: Authors' compilation, SIQSS census monitors and a follow-up, 2000.

of advertising exposure among "learners" and "nonlearners."[14] The figure
indicates that the census campaign can account for as much as a forty-four-
percentage-point increase in the predicted probability of returning the census form: those who recognized no ads and did not know the census is
required by law had a 46 percent predicted likelihood of mail-back cooperation, compared to a 90 percent predicted likelihood of mail-back cooperation among those who recognized all the ads and learned that census
cooperation is required by law during the campaign. Clearly, the mobilization campaign had an impressive impact on census cooperation.

The results here offer striking evidence that the census campaign was
successful. We must always be cautious, of course, in interpreting "campaign effects" because we cannot perfectly isolate the effect of one activity
relative to another. In tracing census knowledge, attitudes, and behavior
over the course of the census campaign, we cannot isolate the effect of a
direct mailing or billboard advertisement from, say, a news report during
the same time period. But because the news stories themselves often
focused on the campaign efforts, the effect undoubtedly traces back to the
public outreach by the Census Bureau.[15]

Given that much of the mobilization campaign was targeted at racial and ethnic minorities, we now assess the extent to which campaign effects differed among various minority groups. Did the mobilization campaign improve cooperation among the hardest-to-count populations, or did it increase census participation only among those groups already likely to cooperate—as the knowledge gap literature suggests (Tichenor, Donohue, and Olien 1970)—thereby increasing the differential undercount? Our earlier descriptive analysis suggested that the campaigns were particularly effective among racial minorities, but does this remain the case when we control for other predictive factors? Although the model in table 2.3 included controls for race/ethnicity, we now include interaction terms between race and census exposure (the advertising recognition measure). This allows us to test whether campaign exposure was particularly effective at increasing census cooperation among minorities.

The full set of coefficients, standard errors, and model fit statistics are reported in model 2 in table 2A.1. Reported in table 2.4 are the advertising exposure coefficients for each population group. Although we find that the main effects for the individual minority groups all remain negative (see table 2A.1), indicating that whites were more likely to return their form if not exposed to any census advertising, the interaction terms between advertising recognition and African Americans and Hispanics are positive and statistically significant. In other words, the campaign had a significant effect on the census cooperation levels of blacks and Hispanics. The interactions show that increasing census advertising recognition increases the probability of census mail-back cooperation among blacks and Hispanics, two groups specifically targeted by the census advertising campaign. In contrast, advertising exposure did not have a significant effect on census cooperation for whites or Asians.

Table 2.4   Census Campaign Exposure Effects from the Multivariate Model, by Race-Ethnicity

Advertising Exposure by Race	Coefficients
Advertising recognition (whites)	.117
African American × ad recognition	.482[†]
Hispanic × ad recognition	.521[†]
Asian American × ad recognition	.122

Source: Authors' compilation, SIQSS census monitors and follow-up, 2000, short form only.
Notes: For full results, see model 2 in table 2A.1. Valid N = 1,274.
[†]$p < .10$

Figure 2.13 illustrates the substantive effects of advertising exposure by race.[16] Among blacks, we see a very dramatic increase in the probability of returning the census form across exposure levels. African Americans who recognized no census ads had a 30.9 percent predicted chance of returning the census form, compared to an 83.1 percent predicted likelihood among those who recognized all four advertising frames—a huge 52.2-percentage-point increase. Likewise, Hispanics who recognized no ads had just a 23.3 percent probability of returning their census form, compared to a 79.5 percent probability among Hispanics with the highest levels of advertising exposure.[17] In contrast, there is a much smaller change in the predicted probability of mail-back cooperation among whites across different levels of census exposure—a change from a 49.4 percent to a 60.9 percent likelihood. One of the most interesting aspects of this prediction is that whites were more likely than minorities to return their census form when they received no campaign exposure, but at the highest levels of campaign exposure blacks and Hispanics were more likely than whites to return their census form. This result suggests that, in direct contrast to the knowledge gap literature (see, for instance, Berinsky 2005), the census

Figure 2.13   The Predicted Effect of Census Ad Recognition, by Race

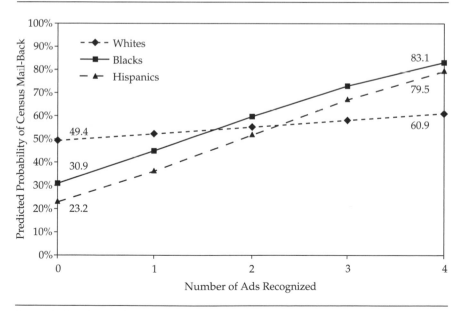

Source: Authors' compilation, SIQSS census monitors and a follow-up, 2000.

mobilization campaign was quite successful in helping to erase the disparities in census participation rates between whites and minorities.

ACTUAL CENSUS COOPERATION

When the final response rates were calculated by the Census Bureau, the 2000 census had not only exceeded the targeted rate but had, contrary to expectations, actually improved upon the 1990 rate. The bureau estimated a 66 percent mail-back response rate, exceeding the 61 percent rate from 1990. This success also translated into a census that was conducted at approximately $500 million less than what was budgeted.

In fact, census cooperation was significantly better than the Census Bureau could report to the public in April 2000. The denominator for the initial mail-back response rate is the number of addresses to which a form is delivered. At the time of the census, the master address file includes an unknown number of vacant houses and apartments. When the bureau has completed all of its many quality checks, it determines how many addresses in the file represent occupied households. With this figure as the denominator, it calculates a final *return* rate.[18] In 2000 the return rate was 78.4 percent, well over three percentage points higher than the comparable number in 1990, and thereby approaching the "plus 5 percent" standard that thousands of communities across the country had adopted. The reported mail-back rate in our data is, of course, a return rate (because all households in the SIQSS sample are, by definition, occupied). Among our respondents, 82.5 percent (margin of error of +/– 3 percentage points) said that they (or their household) returned the census form, an estimate that likely reflects a small overreporting bias.[19]

On our first major question, then, it is clear that public cooperation with the census in 2000 significantly improved. What about the differential undercount? It too showed remarkable improvement in 2000 compared to 1990. Table 2.5 compares the undercounts in 1990 and 2000 for the major minority groups. The African American undercount was reduced by more than half, and for Asians, Hispanics, and Native Americans, the undercount vanished. To be sure, there remained a differential undercount because the white population was overcounted by 1.13 percent (producing a 3 percent differential for blacks, who were undercounted by 1.84 percent). This differential undercount was lower than reported in 1990, but not insignificant either statistically or substantively. Overall, the Census Bureau, after two years of evaluating the 2000 census, reported an estimated net census overcount of half a percent. The census had counted 5.8 million people twice and had missed 4.5 million people, for a net overcount of 1.3 million (Citro et al. 2004, 240–58). Although our data do not speak to this over-

Table 2.5   Undercount of Minorities in the 1990 and 2000 Census

	Percentage Undercounted	
Minority	1990	2000
African American	4.57%	1.84%
Asian	2.36	n.s.
Hispanic	4.99	n.s.
Native Indian	12.20	n.s.

Source: U.S. Census Bureau, 1990 and 2000.
Notes: Rates for both 1990 and 2000 are based on post-enumeration surveys. n.s. = calculated rates are not statistically different from zero.

count, the "success" of the mobilization campaign at reaching and motivating the public may bear some of the responsibility. Children in joint-custody families are often counted twice, as are college students who live away from home and are counted both in their dormitory and by their parents. Two-home families get two forms, and it is easy for one member of the family to return the census form sent to the weekend house without knowing that another member of the family has already reported on a different form. These duplicate errors plague every census and can be aggravated by a campaign insisting that everyone cooperate for the good of the community.

CONCLUSIONS

In contrast to decades of research concluding that political and public health campaigns are generally ineffective, we find that the census campaign efforts were exceptionally successful at informing and mobilizing the American public. Moreover, our analysis suggests that a well-designed and carefully targeted campaign can disproportionately engage and motivate population groups that would otherwise opt out. Minorities who were less likely to cooperate with the census in previous counts were given strong and persuasive reasons to do so in 2000. This differential success among minorities is perhaps one of the most notable (and laudable) findings regarding the census mobilization campaign, especially because previous research has concluded that information campaigns typically increase the gap between the advantaged and disadvantaged.[20] In their seminal work, Philip Tichenor, George Donohue, and Clarence Olien (1970, 159–60) explain this "knowledge gap theory": "As the infusion of mass media information into a social system increases, segments of the population with higher socioeconomic status tend to acquire this information at a faster rate than the lower status segments, so that the gap in knowledge between these segments tends to increase rather than decrease." Subsequent research has found similar gaps with respect to political participation (Eveland and Scheufele 2000). The knowledge gap logic predicted, paradoxically, that census campaign efforts would increase disparities between whites and minorities.[21] Yet our analysis finds dramatic decreases in inequalities in census mail-back cooperation with the infusion of census information. Although we are not the first to challenge the knowledge gap hypothesis (see Ettema, Brown, and Luepker 1983), there is perhaps no more striking example of the extent to which an information campaign can reverse the gap between the advantaged and disadvantaged than the census campaign. Our analysis also gives further credence to the research that suggests that the influence of an information campaign on the knowledge gap depends on information relevance, motivation, and interest (for example, Yanovitzky and Stryker 2001). As our results demonstrate, the census media campaign was particularly successful at capturing the attention and interest of blacks and Hispanics.

On the basis of the findings in this chapter, we conclude that the American population can be mobilized for civic cooperation. There are obvious reasons, however, to resist the temptation to generalize the findings of this chapter to other areas of citizenship, such as voting. For starters, the census is mandatory. And though failure to cooperate is not met with legal action, the mandatory status of census compliance signals the seriousness attached to it—much as is the case with jury duty. Moreover, other special factors were at play in the 2000 census. There was the unusual mix of political forces that led to an unprecedented investment of public monies in the census outreach program. Those factors were census-specific and not transferrable to other areas of public life. In fact, there is no guarantee that the 2010 census will employ a similar outreach effort. Nor can we assume that such an effort would be as effective if it were repeated, an issue we return to in our concluding chapter. In 2000, for instance, the intense focus on the differential undercount reflected a concern that had been building across previous censuses and had led to an all-out effort to "fix it." The (partial)[22] success in 2000 will make it difficult to sustain this focus in 2010 if the stimulus (and panic) regarding the differential undercount has weakened, especially as concerns about the census shift to the duplicates and the overcount that surfaced in 2000.

The accomplishment in 2000 was unprecedented and largely unexpected. It would have been greater yet had it not been for an unanticipated problem that emerged in 2000, one that worked contrary to the effort that went into increasing cooperation. This is the story of the next chapter.

APPENDIX

Table 2A.1   Logistic Regression Results: Effects of Census Campaign
Exposure on Census Cooperation in 2000

	(1)	(2)
Demographics		
Female	.656***	.668***
Age	.091**	.090**
Age squared	.000	.000
Years of education	.002	.004
African American	−.315	−.780*
Hispanic	−.579*	−1.172**
Asian American	−.868†	−.998
R is married	.324†	.360†
R lives in a rural area	.066	.065
R lives in a central city	.366†	.352†
R works at least part-time	.720**	.676**
Census exposure and knowledge		
Number of ads recognized	.217**	.117
Census knowledge (in monitor)[a]	1.813***	1.850***
Change in census knowledge	1.464***	1.461***
Interactions		
African American × ad recognition		.482†
Hispanic × ad recognition		.521†
Asian American × ad recognition		.122
(Constant)	−3.180***	−3.058***
Nagelkerke R^2	.28	.28
Percentage predicted correctly	85.8	86.4
Model chi-square	220.4***	226.5***
(d.f.)	14	17
Change in model chi-square	79.4***	6.1
(d.f.)	2	3

Source: Authors' compilation, SIQSS census monitors and follow-up, 2000, short form only.
Valid N = 1,274.
[a]R knows law requires census participation (measured in individual monitor surveys and
follow-up survey).
***$p < .001$; **$p < .01$; *$p < .05$; †$p < .10$

Chapter Three | Privacy Concerns and Census Cooperation

EVERY TWENTY YEARS the constitutionally mandated decennial census in the United States falls on a presidential election year. In 2000, just as the census mail-back phase got underway, the census became briefly embroiled in the partisan rancor of the heated political environment. Given the broad and bipartisan support for the census mobilization campaign, the Census Bureau had not anticipated such intense and politically charged criticism directed at the census long form, which had just reached one-sixth of America's households. The criticism was focused on the issue of privacy and the question of whether the census long form was an unwarranted government intrusion.

When the privacy debate erupted suddenly, not only was it loud and widespread, but it presented the Census Bureau with an unexpected management crisis at the exact point when census operations were at their most vulnerable. The first complaint came from conservative talk show hosts and editorial writers. Late night comics were quick to chime in, as did political leaders, from small-town mayors to a presidential candidate. George W. Bush told the press that he understood "why people don't want to give over that information to the government. If I had the long form, I'm not so sure I would do it either" (*Albany Times Union* 2000). The Senate got into the act, passing a nonbinding resolution urging that "no American be prosecuted, fined, or in any way harassed by the federal government" for not answering certain questions on the census long form. The Senate was in effect telling the public it was acceptable to ignore what had always been a legal obligation—to complete the census form, short or long.

More generally, with elections approaching, Republican politicians were quick to denounce the census long form as a violation of privacy. The census became a poster child for an "invasive federal government." Congressman Robert W. Schaffer (R-Colo.), who received the long form, said he found some questions "too nosy." Saying he would not answer all of them, Schaffer added: "I'm happy to voluntarily cooperate with the government in areas where I decide it makes sense. Beyond that, it starts to meet the definition of intrusive." The Republican Senate majority leader, Trent Lott (R-Miss.), urged voters to skip any questions they felt violated their privacy. His Senate colleague Chuck Hagel (R-Neb.) similarly advised the public to "just fill out what you need to fill out, and [not] anything you don't feel comfortable with." Republican Tom Coburn of Oklahoma said he was "appalled and outraged by the intrusiveness" of the long-form questions. He argued that "it is ridiculous for the Census Bureau to ask personal questions that have nothing to do with their constitutional mandate to count the citizens of the United States" (Cohn 2000). Six congressional bills were introduced (none passed) that would have seriously affected the ability of the Census Bureau to collect long-form data, an indication of how much attention was drawn to the controversy.

These strong criticisms of the census were widely covered by the press, but that in itself does not tell us what the public heard or how it reacted. Did the privacy controversy depress cooperation with the census? If so—and we report in this chapter that it did—was this only among those who received the long form or was it among the general population? And did it affect recipients' willingness to return the long form in its entirety, or did it more often lead them to skip questions they considered intrusive, as the politicians were recommending?

We proceed in two steps: first, with survey and experimental data we directly link the privacy controversy and reported census behavior; second, and necessarily more inferentially, we consider whether actual census behavior, as reported by the Census Bureau, was influenced by the privacy outcry.

From the perspective of mass communication theories, especially the framing literature described earlier, the eruption of the privacy controversy at the height of the mobilization campaign offers a fascinating case of a strongly positive frame being confronted with a strongly negative one—the first urging cooperation and the second offering reasons not to cooperate. Both messages, as seen by the public, had the endorsement of political leaders, though the negative message was more selectively endorsed. The criticism of the census was voiced almost exclusively by Republicans and conservative media, whereas the mobilization campaign had bipartisan endorsement. In this chapter, we assess the relative impact of these conflicting messages.

Although the dual messages were focused on the census, they had somewhat different objects: the census mobilization campaign targeted census mail-back cooperation more generally, while the privacy debate focused on the long form. It is our working hypothesis, however, that this distinction was lost for most of the general public. We expect to find that overall census cooperation, not just long-form cooperation, was affected by the negative message.

We assess the effect of the debate using a variety of analytic approaches and datasets. As in chapter 2, we track over-time changes in privacy opinions using the SIQSS (Stanford Institute for the Quantitative Study of Society) monitoring surveys; though privacy questions are included in these surveys, at the time of the design we did not fully appreciate the prominence that privacy issues would assume in the census.[1] When the privacy debate erupted in April 2000, we fielded a separate survey focused specifically on the privacy controversy. We also developed an experimental design that was administered after the controversy had fallen from the public eye.[2]

While analyzing the SIQSS tracking data, we limit our analysis to those respondents who received the short form, in keeping with the analysis from chapter 2. In contrast, the experimental data deal explicitly with the long form. Similar results from both studies confirm that the general public in fact did not differentiate between criticisms of the long-form and census-taking more generally. We turn to our findings after providing background on the controversy surrounding the long form during the 2000 census.

THE CENSUS LONG FORM IN 2000

The census long form should be seen in the context of a nearly insatiable appetite in America for information of all kinds. Information is the infrastructure of the emerging "knowledge economy" no less than ports, canals, and railroads were the needed transportation infrastructure for the national industrial economy that displaced a small-scale rural economy in the second half of the nineteenth century. Government agencies and commercial enterprises have a large and ever increasing need for information from and about the American public. The World Association of Opinion and Marketing Research estimates that market research alone topped more than $6 billion. For the federal government, seventy federal agencies collect survey data, at a cost of $5 billion annually. States and even local governments not only are heavy consumers of the federal data but add to it with their own data collection programs. The decennial census, especially the long form, is by far the largest source of easily available information on population and housing characteristics in the United States.

The long-form questionnaire is sent to one of every six households. The remaining households receive the short form, which asks only a few questions, including the age, sex, and race/ethnicity of household members. The short form takes only a few minutes to complete, even for large households. The long form is a lengthy questionnaire; the Census 2000 version included fifty-three main questions and additional follow-up questions. At more than fifty pages, printed on both sides, the questionnaire resembled a small booklet. (The questionnaire had space for up to six household members.)

Beyond the questions on the short form, the long-form demographic questions include questions on ancestry and national origin, marital status, education, languages spoken, place of birth, citizenship, length of residence, physical and mental disabilities, children and grandchildren, military service, occupation and employment history, income, and travel time to work. Questions also cover housing characteristics: size and type of housing, plumbing and kitchen facilities, annual utilities expenses, home ownership, mortgage and taxes, property value, and cost of insurance. Although it is estimated to take less than an hour to complete—and much less time than that in a household of only one or two persons—the long form, in the parlance of survey research, is a "very high burden" questionnaire.

Data from the long form are used to design, manage, and evaluate hundreds of government programs at the national, state, and local levels, ranging from transportation planning to hospital location, from funding school construction to designing emergency evacuation systems. Each year $200 billion in federal funds is distributed on the basis of formulas using long-form information—or $2 trillion across the ten-year life of the data. Each census question fulfills a requirement specified in a federal law or court ruling. Topics to be covered in the long form are submitted to Congress for review, and the actual wording of every question is then resubmitted approximately two years before the census is fielded.

Nevertheless, the reason for asking some of the questions is not transparent. For example, respondents are asked about household plumbing, and whether they have "a sink with piped water, a range or stove, and a refrigerator." Federal agencies use the data to identify places eligible for public assistance programs; local public health officials use this information to locate areas that may be "hot spots" for air or ground water contamination. Another favored target on talk radio was a question about whether any household member has difficulty "dressing, bathing, or getting around inside the home." These data on physical and mental disabilities fulfill the statutory requirements of the Americans with Disabilities Act on matters such as accessible public transportation and, in combination with a question on veteran status, aid in determining the location of VA hospitals. Similarly, data elicited from questions on income, employment, and housing costs are important to economic analysis, especially when combined with data from other large-scale surveys conducted by the government, such as the Consumer Price survey.

The long-form data are as widely used outside of government as they are by the government. Quality information is a public good, and much effort goes into its dissemination in formats accessible to commercial firms, the nonprofit sector, the media, and social scientists whose research helps to show the country where it has been and where it might be going. There are several commercial firms whose sole purpose is converting census data into marketable products.

All of this points to the obvious—a knowledge society thrives on information and expects the government to provide a quality census as the keystone of a population-based information system. Why then were pundits and politicians willing to attack the census? Because the nation's appetite for information conflicts with the public's right to privacy.

Scholars differ on whether the Constitution specifically protects privacy beyond the prohibitions noted in the Fourth Amendment. Privacy was an issue famously framed by the Senate as it debated whether to confirm the nomination of Robert Bork to the Supreme Court. Then the senator from New York, Patrick Moynihan, explained his vote against Bork's appointment: "It is his restricted vision of privacy which troubles me most. I cannot vote for a jurist who simply cannot find in the Constitution a general right to privacy" (Congressional Record 1987, 14011–12). When Bork was rejected by the Senate, Anthony Kennedy was nominated. In his testimony before the Senate Judiciary Committee, which would confirm him unanimously, Kennedy insisted "that the concept of liberty in the due process clause is quite expansive, quite sufficient, to protect the values of privacy that Americans legitimately think are part of their constitutional heritage" (Congressional Record 1988, 728). Whether Moynihan and Kennedy got the Constitution right is not our issue; certainly they were correct, as Kennedy put it, that Americans consider privacy to be part of their constitutional heritage.

It was this heritage, claimed the critics, that was at stake in Census 2000. If information is central to a functioning democracy and economy, so is privacy, and we expect government to protect it rather than infringe on it. Across American history there has been an unspoken but working consensus that it is possible to have both population-based information and privacy protection. Essentially the government has avoided the inherent contradiction by saying to the public, "Yes, you give up a bit of privacy in answering government questions, but this pledge we make to you: If you cooperate, we will never share your answers. They are confidential."

In fact, the pledge of confidentiality is one that the Census Bureau is extremely careful to honor and on which it can point to a remarkable track record. But confidentiality protection and respect for privacy, though closely associated concepts that are often used interchangeably, are not exactly the same thing. The distinction between privacy and confidentiality was drawn by the government in 1971, when the President's Commission on Federal Statistics defined privacy as "the individual's right to decide whether and to what extent he will divulge to the government his thoughts, opinions, feelings, and the facts of his personal life" and defined confidentiality as prohibiting disclosure "of data in a manner that would allow public identification of the respondent or would in any way be harmful to him" (President's Commission on Federal Statistics 1971, 197, 222).

This is the distinction between intrusiveness and disclosure, between "don't ask" and "don't tell." Saying "I won't answer that question because it is none of your business" reflects a privacy concern. In contrast, saying "I won't answer that question because you may share it without my knowledge or permission" reflects a confidentiality concern. We cannot make too much of this conceptual distinction, however, for several reasons, one being that it is hard to know when a "leave me alone" response is motivated by a mistrust of how the government might use the information. Public discourse blurs the distinction, as does the survey data available to us. But before turning to the data, we would remind the reader that the substance of the 2000 controversy focused on privacy more than confidentiality. The rhetoric used by Republican politicians makes this clear—the Senate resolution, for instance, made no reference to disclosure issues, emphasizing instead "objectionable questions." The issue was perhaps best framed by the Libertarian Party in a widely cited statement: "Real Americans don't answer nosy Census questions. You can strike a blow for privacy, equality, and liberty by refusing to answer every question on the Census form except the one required by the Constitution: How many people live in your home?" (*The Columbian* 2000).

THE PUBLIC REACTION TO THE PRIVACY CONTROVERSY

As we outlined earlier, current mass communication theory holds that elite or media messages primarily influence mass opinion by shaping and formulating the issues we think about and how we think about them (Iyengar 1991). By framing an issue in a particular way, the same values and facts are stressed over others and endowed with greater apparent relevance than they would have under an alternative frame (Nelson, Clawson, and Oxley 1997). The Census Bureau spent millions of dollars to frame the census in terms of civic participation, emphasizing the community benefits of cooperation. The census critics who cited privacy concerns framed the census as unnecessarily intrusive, implying that the government did not actually need the information it was collecting. To characterize the census in this way casts a negative light on the entire enterprise.

Theory tells us that the extent to which frames are persuasive depends not only on the intensity or reach of the message but also on whether those frames resonate with existing predispositions in the public (Zaller 1992). In this context, the mobilization campaign was effective because the public was positively predisposed toward the census. By the same token, we would expect the negative framing to be influential if there were preexisting public concerns about government intrusiveness.

There is ample reason to expect such preexisting attitudes. Both a real and a perceived loss of privacy are associated with the vast information collected about the American public. Government and businesses use data aggregated from millions of individual characteristics that come from the census, from surveys, from administrative records, and increasingly from surveillance systems that record behaviors ranging from supermarket choices to Internet sites visited, from library books checked out to passes through electronic tollbooths. The rise in sophisticated computer connectivity offers the technical ability to link these various types of information to build individual profiles. Although the census and government statistical surveys are not included in these information broker systems, this is not well understood by the public.

Whether the resulting loss in privacy is judged by citizens to be an acceptable trade-off for improved social services, better products, and enhanced homeland security is a large empirical question waiting to be answered. Kent Walker (2000, 2) describes these trade-offs:

> Withholding personal information from others keeps you from enjoying all that society and the market have to offer. . . . It means that you'll get less junk mail (and fewer offers of possible interest to you), that Amazon.com won't track which books you prefer (or be able to suggest new ones of interest to you), that Safeway won't track your buying patterns (or give you discounts in exchange), that cameras won't observe you walking down the street (or catch red-light-runners), or that other people won't know about your interests (or be able to engage you in e-mail chats about them).

However the trade-off is eventually made, Americans approach it with wariness. More than eight of every ten Americans now believe that businesses or people they do not know will gain access to personal information about them (Fox et al. 2000). In the years preceding the 2000 census, privacy concerns had been steadily increasing. A compilation of polls by Alan Westin found that fewer than one-third (31 percent) of Americans said they were "very" concerned about threats to privacy in 1978. By 1998 this number had climbed to 55 percent, and in the census year of 2000 to 69 percent (Westin 2000). In a 2001 online Harris interactive survey, half of the respondents felt that they did not have an appropriate level of control over how their personal information is collected and used by companies. Another 2001 study reported that only two in five Americans agreed that "organizations that conduct polls/surveys can be trusted to protect my rights to privacy"—a decline of eleven percentage points since 1995 (Bowers 2001). And in a Harris survey that asked respondents to define the aspects of privacy that were most important to them, the top response was "not being disturbed at home": more than half the respondents (55 percent) said this was "extremely important," and an additional 35 percent said it was "somewhat important."

As noted in chapter 1, privacy concerns have lessened public cooperation with government and private-sector surveys. Figure 3.1 displays the rapid growth over the last twenty years in the percentage of the American population who reported that they had refused to answer at least one survey in the past year. Obviously these numbers underestimate the refusal rates because they are based on responses from persons who cooperated with this survey in the first place.

Figure 3.1   Survey Refusal Trend in Past Year, 1980 to 2001

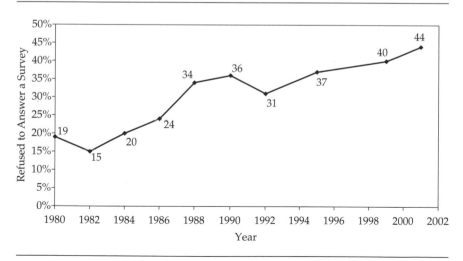

Source: Sheppard (2001). Reprinted with permission from the Council for Marketing Opinion and Research.

Research has also found that concerns about confidentiality are related to census cooperation. Robert Fay, Nancy Bates, and Jeffrey Moore (1991) examined and compared the relationship between privacy and confidentiality items and census cooperation in 1980 and 1990. They report that although the percentage of the population trusting the Census Bureau's pledge of confidentiality was constant (73 and 79 percent of people agreed that census confidentiality could be trusted in the postcensus evaluation in 1980 and 1990, respectively), there was a significant change in the relationship between levels of trust and the self-reported census return rate. In 1990 those with positive attitudes on all three items were significantly more likely to return the census form, while there was no relationship between trust and census cooperation in 1980. In other words, even those individuals who did not trust census confidentiality were no less likely to complete their census forms (although perhaps begrudgingly) in 1980, but by 1990 those who did not trust census confidentiality were significantly less likely to cooperate. Elizabeth Martin (2001, 31), in an analysis of data from the 2000 Census Monitoring Study and the 1990 Outreach Evaluation Survey, found "several indications that Census 2000 engendered more sensitivity and a more diverse privacy reaction than the previous census." Other studies also conclude that both privacy concerns and negative views about the federal government have contributed to census nonresponse (Mayer 2002; Bulmer 1979). In the most comprehensive treatment, Eleanor Singer, Nancy Mathiowetz, and Mick Couper (1993) report a significant relationship between mail response and confidentiality concerns in the 1990 census. Singer and her colleagues John Van Howeyk and Randall Neugebauer repeated the study after the 2000 census and again found that concerns about confidentiality and privacy depressed census return rates (Singer et al. 2003). These studies suggest that drawing the attention of the public to the census as unwarranted government intrusiveness might very well dampen positive attitudes about the census (Weakliem and Villemez 2004). We assess the extent to which the privacy debate found a receptive American public and whether the negative rhetoric had an impact on census attitudes and cooperation.

MEASURING THE EFFECTS OF THE PRIVACY CONTROVERSY

Because the privacy controversy erupted just as American households were being asked to mail back their census forms, we have a real-world event that can inform us about the comparative influence of a strongly positive message ("The census is good for you and your community") versus a strongly negative one ("The census violates your privacy"). We assess the impact of the privacy debate with three distinct analytic approaches. With the SIQSS monitoring studies, we track over-time changes in privacy views. As the privacy controversy erupted, we conducted an independent cross-sectional survey to assess the influence of the controversy and respondents' awareness of it. Finally, we designed an experiment that allowed direct comparison of the impact of negative and positive framing on long-form completion. We take up each of these data sources in turn.

Privacy Concerns and Census Cooperation

From the SIQSS monitoring surveys, we graph in figure 3.2 changes in the level of agreement with the following statements: (1) "My answers to the census could be used against me"; (2) "The Census Bureau promise of confidentiality cannot be trusted"; and (3) "The census is an invasion of privacy." Despite the successful reach of the positive advertising campaign and other mobilization programs, all three measures of privacy concerns increased over the course of the census data collection period. There was

Figure 3.2   Privacy Concerns over Time

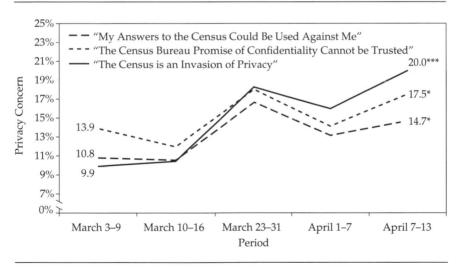

Source: Authors' compilation, SIQSS census monitors, 2000.

Notes: Percentage of those agreeing or strongly agreeing to a privacy concern. Significance levels apply for the increase from March 3–9 to April 7–13. N = 980 (March 3–9); 960 (March 10–16); 650 (March 23–31); 940 (April 1–7); 880 (April 7–13).
*** p < .001; * p < .05.

an initial small decline in the second week of March as the advertising campaign got into full swing, but by early April (during the fifth monitoring survey), when the Census Bureau was anxiously watching the rate at which census forms were being returned, 20 percent of respondents agreed or strongly agreed that the census was an invasion of privacy, 18 percent believed that the Census Bureau promise of confidentiality could not be trusted, and 15 percent feared that "my answers to the census could be used against me."

Trust in the pledge of confidentiality did not move much across the five monitor surveys, indicating that the public had made up its mind on the issue of confidentiality before the census got under way. In contrast, the number of those indicating that "the census is an invasion of privacy" increased as the long form arrived and the privacy controversy first hit the press, as did concerns that census answers "could be used against me," although to a somewhat lesser extent. It appears, then, that the public did react to the privacy debate. However, was census behavior itself affected?

To assess the effect of privacy concerns we estimate a multivariate logistic regression model of census mail-back cooperation (a dichotomous variable), which we predict as a function of privacy measures, mobilization campaign exposure, and demographic controls, including gender, age, education, race, marital status, work status, and urban/rural geography. Because the privacy debate had a partisan dimension, we also include measures of party affiliation and political ideology, combining these variables to construct five groups: liberal and moderate Democrats, conservative and moderate Republicans, and a baseline that includes independents, moderate partisans, and cross-pressured partisans (liberal Republicans and conservative Democrats).[3] We capture the effect of the privacy debate by including, in addition to a baseline measure of privacy attitudes, a measure of *change* in privacy attitudes during the privacy controversy by comparing respondents' reported privacy concerns from the follow-up survey with their reported privacy concerns from the monitoring surveys.[4] It is impossible, of course, to directly link changes in privacy attitudes to the elite-level debate, since we cannot perfectly isolate the effects of news coverage of the controversy from, say, discussions with a coworker at the water cooler. However, given the high profile of the controversy, we assume that all changes in opinion can be attributed at least indirectly to the "privacy debate."

The key findings are reported in table 3.1, and the full set of coefficients, standard errors, and model fit statistics can be found in table 3A.1. The results are consistent with studies of the 1990 and 2000 censuses—privacy concerns are related to lower levels of census cooperation. The coefficient for privacy concerns is negative and statistically significant, indicating that

Table 3.1   The Effect of the Privacy Debate on Census
            Cooperation in 2000

	Logit Coefficient
Census campaign exposure	
Number of ads recognized	.233**
R knows law requires one to participate in census (measured in monitor)	1.714***
Change in knowing that law requires one to answer census questions	1.374***
Privacy concerns	
Census is invasion of privacy (measured in monitor)	−2.179***
Change in privacy concern between monitor and follow-up	−1.236**

Source: Authors' compilation, SIQSS census monitors and follow-up, 2000, short form only.
Note: Valid N = 1,235. For full results, see appendix.
**p < .01; ***p < .001

higher initial levels of privacy concerns are associated with lower levels of census mail-back cooperation. More notably, however, individuals whose privacy concerns increased while privacy issues were being loudly debated were even less likely to mail back their census form. Privacy concerns that were heightened over the course of the census collection period had a larger negative impact on census mail-back cooperation than preexisting concerns. The privacy controversy sparked by talk shows, editorials, political speeches, and the like depressed census cooperation rates by reinforcing, heightening, and even creating privacy concerns. These findings offer quite clear evidence that the privacy debate primed privacy considerations as the public decided whether to cooperate with the census.[5]

Although our findings indicate that the negative rhetoric was persuasive, we are also interested in the effect of the privacy debate relative to the positive influence of the mobilization campaign. The results reported in table 3.1 show that our census campaign exposure measures, the number of census advertisements recognized, and changes in census knowledge over the campaign still have a positive and significant effect on census mail-back cooperation. In other words, greater exposure to the census campaign was related to higher levels of census cooperation. Thus, even the loud and sustained outcry about the intrusiveness of the long form could not wash out the positive impact of the mobilization efforts.

The substantive impact of the privacy coefficients on census cooperation can be seen more clearly in figure 3.3. This figure uses the coefficients

Figure 3.3   The Predicted Effects of Changing Attitudes Toward Privacy Among Those with No Such Concern in Initial Survey

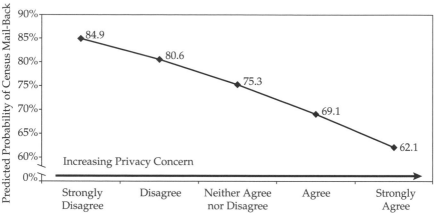

Do You Agree that the Census Is an Invasion of Privacy? (Measured in June 2000)

Source: Authors' compilation, SIQSS monitors and follow-up, 2000.
Notes: Privacy concern is measured in monitors (initial privacy concern) and in follow-up (May 12–June 12) as one item: "Do you agree that the census is an invasion of privacy?" The chart shows the cooperation rates for those who initially strongly disagreed with the statement.

estimated in table 3.1 to calculate the likelihood of census cooperation among those respondents who entered the census period not seeing the census as an invasion of privacy but who came to have privacy concerns during the public controversy.[6] If these initially unconcerned individuals remained unconcerned throughout the debate, the model predicts a 85 percent likelihood of census cooperation. In contrast, for individuals who change from being unconcerned to later strongly agreeing that the census is an invasion of privacy, the model predicts a 62 percent likelihood of cooperation. This 23 percentage-point drop in predicted cooperation illustrates the sizable negative priming effect. The controversy, above and beyond any respondent's initial concerns about privacy, had a large and direct impact on cooperation levels in the 2000 census. We emphasize that this analysis was restricted to individuals who received the census short form (for comparability with previous analysis). Even though the census criticism was targeted toward the census long form, the analysis indicates that the privacy debate depressed cooperation for the short form as well (Junn 2001).

Privacy Concerns and Completing the Census Form   Although our attention has been focused primarily on whether Americans returned their census forms, there is a second dimension of cooperation. We next ask whether the privacy controversy led to high rates of item nonresponse (skipping questions)—that is, respondents returning the form but leaving it incompletely filled out. The repeated negative message did not focus on whether to mail the form back but rather on whether to ignore "intrusive" questions. To again cite the advice from the Libertarian Party: "Strike a blow for privacy, equality, and liberty by refusing to answer every question on the Census form except the one required by the Constitution: How many people live in your home?" To follow this advice would be to mail a form back to the Census Bureau having left most of it blank. Thus, we are interested in the effects of the privacy controversy on census *completion*.

Our first evidence of the effect of the census controversy on census completion comes from a separate cross-sectional survey fielded shortly after the long-form controversy emerged. Over the weekend of April 1, 1,933 new respondents were briefly surveyed about the long-form controversy. In this sample, 18 percent (339) had received the long-form questionnaire from the Census Bureau, while 67 percent (1,297) reported getting the short form. (The remaining 15 percent of the sample either did not know which Census 2000 form their household received or said they did not get a form.)

Confirming our multivariate results from the SIQSS monitoring surveys, we find that there was substantial awareness about the privacy controversy. Nearly half of short-form recipients (48 percent) and more than half of long-form recipients (54 percent) said that they had heard about the debate about census questions. Of those familiar with the controversy, more than one-third (35 percent) reported that it made them feel less like answering all of the questions.

The controversy was more salient for those who received the long form. Among this group, nearly half (48 percent) reported that what they saw or heard about the controversy made them feel less like answering all of the questions. A smaller proportion (29 percent) of short-form recipients conveyed the same sentiment. We asked: "Do you think that the questions in the census long form are too intrusive and shouldn't be asked?" Nearly half (47 percent) of long-form recipients said that the questions were too intrusive, while fewer than one-quarter of those who received the short form (22 percent) agreed. It is impossible to tell whether this difference is due to more knowledge of the actual questions among those who received the long form or simply the perception of the burden of filling out a fifty-page booklet. At the same time 38 percent of long-form recipients said that the questions were not too intrusive and that the census needed to ask the questions.

The survey results confirm our earlier conclusion that the negative rhetoric probably had a depressing effect on cooperation. And there is also indication that the controversy may have had an even greater impact on census completion than on the census mail-back cooperation already documented. This is intuitively persuasive. Census cooperation is mandatory, but that obligation can be fulfilled by returning a half-completed form. And the controversy was never about cooperation as such, but about intrusive questions. Although we do not have a sufficient number of cases to run a separate multivariate analysis from our tracking data on only those who received the long form, we developed an experiment to assess directly the impact of the controversy on questionnaire completion.

A month after the widely covered controversy about privacy and long-form questions, we administered an intricate experimental survey that included three-quarters of the questions from the actual Census 2000 long form.[7] The survey was a random sample of 2,000 individuals who had not participated in the SIQSS monitoring survey. Each respondent was asked which census form their household received, and only the 1,213 respondents who received the short form were included in the experiment. (Receiving the long form from the Census Bureau was a learning experience that would have compromised answers to the experiment.) These respondents were randomly assigned to one of two treatment groups or a control group. In addition to the questions from the census long form, we included a number of attitudinal items about the census at the end of the survey.

One treatment group was positively primed by a presentation of information about the many important uses of census data. The other group was negatively primed with a series of questions that asked whether they agreed with people who refused to answer questions they found intrusive, whether they thought some census questions were a violation of privacy, and whether they thought people should skip questions with which they felt uncomfortable. This treatment echoed the negative rhetoric of some politicians during the long-form controversy in April (see actual experiment wording in the appendix).

We examine three issues—the number of questions skipped, the types of questions skipped, and attitudes about the census and the long form in particular. From table 3.2, which shows the proportion of questions skipped for the three groups, we can see that the negative stimulus had a significant influence on question-answering behavior.[8] If members of this group skipped questions at all, they were going to skip many more than

Table 3.2   Percentage of Questions Skipped, by Treatment

	Treatment Group		
	Negative	Control	Positive
Average percentage of questions skipped	19%	12%	14%
Skipped 60 percent or more questions	3	1	3
Skipped 30 to 60 percent of questions	24	12	9
Skipped less than 30 percent of questions	73	87	88

Source: Authors' compilation, SIQSS census experiment data, 2000.
Note: We report the percentage of questions skipped because the number of valid questions varies across individuals.

members of either of the other groups. For example, 27 percent of respondents in the negative treatment group skipped more than 30 percent of questions, compared to just 13 percent of control group and 12 percent of positive treatment group.

Somewhat surprisingly, the skip rate of the positive treatment group is not statistically different from that of the control group.[9]

Table 3.3 draws our attention to the next issue—what types of questions are skipped, and does this differ by treatment assignment? As the Census Bureau has reported in the past (see the discussion in the next section), questions are not uniformly skipped by households. It is evident from the results reported in table 3.3 that the most frequently skipped questions are those that are more demanding—answers are either hard to recall or hard to compute—and those that are more sensitive, such as questions about wages and salary. Our primary interest here, however,

Table 3.3   Types of Questions Skipped, by Treatment

	Treatment Group		
	Negative	Control	Positive
Race	4%	3%	2%
Bathroom plumbing	8	3	4
One or more disabilities	15	8	10
Wages and salary	32	21	18
Annual real estate taxes	42	33	35
Annual electricity cost	50	35	44

Source: Authors' compilation, SIQSS census experiment data, 2000.

is in the effect of the experimental treatment. The finding replicates what we saw in table 3.2. Across these questions, excepting the race item, the group receiving the negatively primed treatment has statistically significant higher rates of item nonresponse than those not so primed. Interestingly, some of the questions targeted in the privacy controversy— those about bathroom plumbing and about individuals with disabilities— were much less likely to be skipped than questions about income, taxes, and utility costs.

Again, the patterns between the positively primed group and the control group are not statistically different from each other. Despite being told about the important uses to which census data are put, respondents were no less likely to skip questions than those in the control group. We conclude that negative priming is effective, while a positive message about particular questions is much less so. This finding is consistent with a considerable amount of research on political persuasion suggesting that negative messages are more effective than positive ones (Perloff 2003), but it may also reflect the fact that the public had already received positive messages from the actual census campaign. In other words, the control group and the positive treatment group may not have received very different information. It remains to be seen whether attitudes toward the census are influenced by a positive message. Table 3.4 presents the attitude data across the three groups.

Here the patterns are as initially hypothesized. Respondents who were told how specific census information is used were less likely to endorse question skipping (69 percent) than those whose treatment echoed the public voices insisting that the census violates privacy rights (82 percent); the control group was in the middle (75 percent). A similar expected pattern

Table 3.4   Attitudes, by Treatment Group

	Treatment Group		
	Negative	Control	Positive
"The census has good reasons for all of the questions on the long form."	14%	18%	22%
"Someone should refuse to answer a census question they think is a violation of their privacy."	82	75	69

Source: Authors' compilation, SIQSS census experiment data, 2000.

holds for an item asking whether there are good reasons for the questions on the long form. Nonetheless, the overall percentages are quite dismal.

The experimental data lend additional and strong support to the general conclusion already reached: negative voices during the census-taking phase had an effect on the ability of the Census Bureau to conduct a full and complete census count. The fact that overall census cooperation was less than it otherwise would have been shows up both in mail-back return rates and in item nonresponse. Moving from survey data to a look at what actually happened in the 2000 census adds powerfully to this conclusion.

The Long Form in Census 2000

No census collects 100 percent of the information requested from everyone who returns a form. The Census Bureau uses a statistical imputation technique to fill in missing values. It imputes a value based on the prevailing patterns in the household or neighborhood. The bureau reports these imputation or assignment rates for every question on the census form. There was a slight but worrisome increase in these rates between the 1980 and 1990 censuses. For example, 10 percent of the population skipped the question on wages and salary in 1990, which was a slight increase over the prior census. But earlier experience did not prepare the Census Bureau for the historic high rates of item nonresponse reached in 2000. Nonresponse to the wages and salary question doubled to 20 percent (consistent with the control group in the experimental data). Table 3.5 shows the increase in actual census item nonresponse for eight questions from the long form.

Table 3.5   Imputation and Assignment Rates in 1990 and 2000 Long-Form Censuses

Item	1990	2000
Number of rooms	0.4%	6.2%
Age	0.9	2.6
Marital status	0.9	3.4
Monthly rent	1.3	15.6
Value of property	3.3	13.3
Occupation last year	9.1	16.1
Wage and salary income	10.0	20.0
Property taxes	12.2	32.0

Source: U.S. Census Bureau.

Item nonresponse on even relatively neutral questions, such as age of the household member or the number of rooms in the house, increased many-fold. The question on property taxes was skipped by nearly one-third of the population, up from 12 percent in 1990. Item nonresponse severely weakens the quality of census data, data that are the backbone of policy program design and administration and the basis on which we assess the health of the U.S. economy. More worrisome is the question of whether this trend in nonresponses is a harbinger of worse to come, an issue we return to in chapter 5.

There is an additional fact of relevance to the findings in this chapter. Since the mail-back census was inaugurated, the return rate of the long form has lagged that of the short form, as might be expected given that on average the former takes more than half an hour to complete and the latter only about three minutes. As figure 3.4 shows, this gap was negligible in 1970 and 1980, when it was stable at 2 percent despite the overall decline in census cooperation. There was a further decline in the mail-back rate in 1990, when the gap between the long and short forms widened to 5 percent. It nearly doubled again in 2000, with 9 percent fewer long forms being returned than short forms (Prewitt 2004). Without this growing gap

Figure 3.4   Census Return Rates, 1970 to 2000

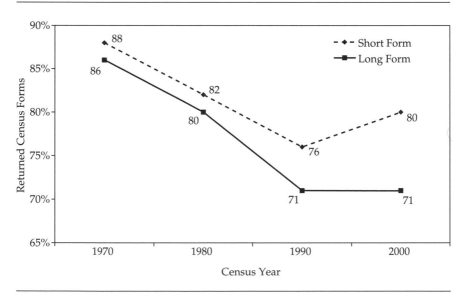

Source: U.S. Census Bureau.

between the short- and long-form return rates, the success in reversing the overall decline in census cooperation, as discussed in chapter 2, would have been even more impressive.[10]

The significant increase in item nonresponse and the evident inability of the mobilization campaign to increase census cooperation uniformly across both short- and long-form households are consistent with the survey results reported in this chapter. The privacy controversy took a toll on the census, contributing to higher census costs by depressing mail-back rates (thus requiring labor-intensive personal follow-up) and contributing to data deterioration by increasing item nonresponse. The toll would no doubt have been much higher had it not been for the positive and highly successful mobilization campaign. As the experimental data suggest, it may be easier to get the American public to return a form than to persuade people to return it completely filled in. No doubt many things influenced the extraordinarily high item nonresponse to the long form, including the thankless nature of the task itself and a growing "leave me alone" attitude in the public. That said, we are left with an important unknown. If the mobilization campaign had emphasized why specific questions are important to the nation's policies and economy, would that have helped to neutralize the powerful negative rhetoric about a threat to privacy rights? Or has the nation come to a point in its collective anxiety about privacy that no amount of public education is likely to make much of a difference if the census again becomes a tantalizing target in 2010? Chapter 5 takes up this question and offers a recommendation that, we believe, could significantly dampen the effect of privacy concerns on census cooperation. First, however, we consider in chapter 4 the differences between civic and political participation and evaluate the impact of social capital on census cooperation in 2000.

APPENDIX

The actual wording of the negative and positive priming treatments during the experiment was as follows:

- Positive priming:
    1. "Every question in Census 2000 is required by law to manage and evaluate programs, and to help distribute $180 billion dollars in federal funds to states and local communities in a fair and equitable way. Are you familiar with the uses of census statistics?" (yes; no; don't know)
    2. "Census statistics on income and employment are used for . . .

        ". . . measuring the general economic health of America.

"... identifying areas needing job training and employment programs.

"... helping produce the figures for the consumer price index."

3. "Census statistics on education are used for ...

"... tracking literacy rates.

"... identifying communities needing more schools."

4. "Census statistics on housing are used for ...

"... comparing housing values across America.

"... assessing the need for housing assistance for the elderly.

"... locating areas in danger of ground water contamination and waterborne disease."

5. "Census statistics on race are used for ...

"... measuring fulfillment of laws, including the Voting Rights Act."

6. "Census statistics on physical disabilities are used for ...

"... identifying areas in need of services for disabled Americans."

- Negative priming:
  1. "The newspaper *USA Today* reported that a growing number of people felt some of the questions on the census long form were too intrusive. Some of these people refused to answer some of the questions. Do you ...

     "... agree with these people's actions?

     "... neither agree nor disagree with their actions?

     "... disagree with these people's actions?"

  2. "Do you think it is a violation of privacy for the government to ask questions on the census long form about things such as income and physical and mental disabilities?" (yes; no; don't know)

  3. "Some people are saying that people should not answer questions they feel uncomfortable with. Do you ...

     "... strongly agree?

     "... agree?

     "... neither agree nor disagree?

     "... disagree?

     "... strongly disagree?"

Table 3A.1   Logistic Regression Results: Effects of Privacy Controversy on Census Cooperation in 2000

	B (Log Odds)
Demographics	
Female	.611**
Age	.090**
Age squared	.000
Years of education	−.027
African American	−.600*
Hispanic	−.740*
Asian American	−1.022†
R is married	.413*
R lives in a rural area	.303
R lives in a central city	.322
R works at least part-time	.847**
Party affiliation or ideology	
Liberal Democrat	.891*
Moderate Democrat	.555*
Moderate Republican	−.472†
Conservative Republican	.407
Mobilization effort	
Number of ads recognized	.233**
Knowledge	
R knows law requires one to participate in census (measured in monitor)	1.714***
Change in knowing that law requires one to answer census questions	1.374***
Privacy concern	
Census is invasion of privacy (measured in monitor)	−2.179***
Change in privacy concern between monitor and follow-up	−1.236**
Constant	−1.978*
Nagelkerke R^2	.32
Predicted correctly	86.5%
Model chi-square	243.5***
N	1,235

Source: Authors' compilation, SIQSS census monitors and follow-up, 2000, short form only.
†p < .10; *p < .05; **p < .01; ***p < .001

Chapter Four | Census Cooperation: Community and Household

CENSUS COOPERATION IS often described as a form of civic engagement. In the media attention surrounding the 2000 census, the decennial count was routinely characterized as a "civic ceremony," one that differs from voting in its nonpartisanship but is similar to voting in that it is a social-political duty that provides important community goods. Because of these parallels, it has long been assumed that the determinants of census cooperation and political participation are similar. Most notably, journalists and scholars have assumed that community involvement (or social capital) predicts census cooperation much as it predicts other forms of civic engagement. In other words, the individuals who vote in elections, volunteer in community organizations, and participate in charitable activities should be more likely to cooperate with the census because of their feelings of civic duty and their commitment to the welfare of their communities. If this assumption is confirmed, we can extrapolate that the long-term decline in community participation has depressed census cooperation and will continue to do so, and consequently, the Census Bureau should focus future mobilization and information campaigns on civic engagement considerations, perhaps borrowing strategies from voter mobilization campaigns. On the other hand, a finding that census participation is *not* predicted by the same community involvement factors that predict political participation would raise questions about theories of civic mobilization and alter the strategies available to the Census Bureau in its efforts to promote cooperation.

The surprising finding is that the relationship between community involvement and census participation is not as strong or straightforward as has been generally assumed. Although community involvement is a strong predictor of other forms of civic participation—namely voting—we find almost no relationship between community involvement and census participation. Rather, we find that basic characteristics *of the household* more strongly predict census mail-back cooperation. This finding has tremendous implications for future censuses. Community involvement can be mobilized and motivated—as was made apparent by the increase in voter turnout in the 2004 presidential election and the spike in charitable contributions and blood donations following the tragedies of September 11, 2001. In contrast, the composition of American households is largely out of the hands of political leaders and policymakers. Changing trends in household and family composition present a difficult challenge to the Census Bureau that will need to be addressed in future censuses.

CENSUS COOPERATION AND COMMUNITY INVOLVEMENT

As discussed in chapter 2, the core message of the 2000 census campaign was focused on community-based benefits, such as better targeting of government funds to needy areas for schools, day care, and other services (Citro et al. 2004, 107).[1] In developing this message, the Census Bureau drew on research indicating that participation in the census, like participation in politics, is affected by an individual's attachment to and sense of civic duty toward the society at large (Bates and Buckley 2000; Couper et al. 1998). Later the Census Bureau commissioned a study of civic attitudes and census cooperation on the premise that census participation is motivated by the same sense of civic duty that predicts community involvement (Crowley 2003, 1). This study concludes that "individuals who engage in civic activities—such as voting, volunteering at soup kitchens and joining political advocacy groups—will most likely participate in Census surveys." Following from that assumption, the report recommends a community-based slogan for the 2010 Census: "Be counted in your community so that you can count on your community. Return your 2010 Census form" (23). The report recommends that future promotional materials for the census "emphasize making a difference through Census participation in one's local community" because participation in the decennial census "is an easy way in which a generation can give back to the community while empowering the community" (vii–viii).

This recommendation echoes the sentiments of Robert Putnam (2000, 142), who has suggested that the decline in census cooperation can be attributed to an overall decline in community involvement in American society. Referencing the disappointing 1990 census cooperation rate, Putnam concludes that cooperation was lowest among those detached from community institutions.[2] On the eve of the 2000 census, he reiterated that census cooperation "is a function of whether [persons] are connected to their communities." Putnam explains: "Basically, there are growing numbers of

Americans who are not connected to their communities in the way their parents were. . . . The people who fail to return the Census forms are not people who are especially upset at Washington. It's not a function of Vietnam or Watergate or Monica. It's a function of whether they are connected to their communities" (Kenworthy 2000).

Other studies, however, have challenged the hypothesis that community involvement is the primary factor predicting census cooperation. Sherman Edwards and Michael Wilson (2003), based on a multivariate analysis of the census marketing effort, recommend that the Census Bureau think twice about the community-based model that underlay the design of the 2000 mobilization campaign.[3] This and other studies hint at the possible importance of household structure. In looking at 1990 census cooperation, for instance, David Word (1997) finds that renters living in spousal households have a significantly lower nonresponse rate (25.4 percent) than renters living in nonspousal households (40.8 percent). Jacob Vigdor (2001) also reports that counties high in female-headed households have lower levels of census cooperation. This suggests that census participation is shaped by a factor considerably more elemental than community engagement—the composition of the household. Part of the explanation may be logistic— more complex household structures are simply more difficult to enumerate on a census form. More generally, the factors that contribute to an individual living in an unconventional household influence the likelihood that he or she will return a census form. In this chapter, we explicitly compare the effect of community involvement and household composition on census cooperation and analyze them as predictors of political participation.

CENSUS COOPERATION AND THE AMERICAN HOUSEHOLD

The decennial census has always been household-based. In 1790 the enumerator asked not "who is in the family" but "who lives here," producing a household count that included servants and slaves as well as family members. Today's census starts with a master address file—unique addresses attached to residential units. As the census gets under way, the Census Bureau knows only that each address is a residential unit and mails the census form to that address, never to an individual. In Census Bureau terminology, a household is composed of one or more people occupying a housing unit, *irrespective* of familial ties. A married commuting couple may think of themselves as a family; for census-taking, however, they are two distinct households, and it is possible that neither one would be considered a family household.

Because not all households contain families, the Census Bureau distinguishes between family and nonfamily households. A family household consists of two or more persons related by marriage, birth, or adoption. Such households can include persons unrelated to the family. Indeed, there can be two (or more) families unrelated to each other sharing the same residence, and yet this household would receive only one census form. Nonfamily households include persons who live alone and those in which unrelated individuals share a residence—the off-campus living quarters of college students being a familiar example. Technically, the decennial census is household-based in the sense that it starts with residential addresses irrespective of how those households-as-residences divide between family and nonfamily households (which of course cannot be determined except by taking the census).

Although the census is household-based, its public face is that of a family-based undertaking. And the census image of family has historically been the traditional nuclear family. The 2000 census advertising portrayed families filling out census forms together, as had been done in all previous decennials. Indeed, Crowley (2003) recommends a family message for future census mobilization campaigns as well, urging the Census Bureau to promote census participation as a family activity and to stress the benefits of the census to families.

Also, the format of the census has historically been family-based. In our earliest censuses, from 1790 to 1840, only the name of the household head—presumed, of course, to be the father of the family living in the household—was collected. Other members were simply enumerated by race, gender, and age. Then for more than a century the census form asked first for the name of the head of household and then for the name of the "wife of head." Under the influence of the feminist movement, in 1980 the census form was directed to the household generally rather than to the "head" of the household. Any member of the household could now fill out the form and specify the relationships among family members. Thus, although across census history the unit of data collection has always been the household, the image and implicit message was that households and families are more or less interchangeable. Of course, the Census Bureau knows that household composition has changed radically in recent decades, but at least through the 2000 census, the household "picture" was still the picture of a family household.

A household-based focus draws attention to the way in which individual responsibility in census cooperation differs in important respects from other types of civic participation. The underlying assumption in the social capital literature is that the proper unit of analysis is the individual. Although influenced by his or her social networks, it is the individual who decides whether to commit to civic participation. To take the clearest example, voting is an individual act. In the same household, the wife might vote and the husband might not, but the wife cannot vote on behalf of the husband. In census-taking the primary unit of data collection, data recording, and data reporting is the household, and no member can opt out. Moreover, any member of the household can and should complete the census on behalf of all household members.[4] You may be able to bowl alone (or vote alone), but unless you live by yourself, you cannot "census alone." You enter the census as a household member.

Proponents of the community-based civic engagement hypothesis have usually ignored family- or household-based variables; in some instances they have even suggested that having a family can reduce community involvement, which by extension, would have a negative effect on census participation. Putnam (2000, 278) reports, for instance, that married people are less likely to spend time informally with neighbors and friends, since "married people tend to be homebodies." He likewise finds that being a parent tends to reduce membership in some organizations; only membership in church and school-related organizations is positively related to marriage. He concludes that "holding other demographic features constant, marriage and children are *negatively* correlated with membership in sports, political, and cultural groups, and they are simply unrelated to membership in business and professional groups, service clubs, ethnic organizations, neighborhood associations, and hobby groups. Married people attend *fewer* club meetings than demographically matched single people" (278). Based on Putnam's analysis, therefore, we might expect to find that "traditional family" variables actually reduce census cooperation, at least if community participation is a determinant of whether a household returns the form. In the next section, we attempt to sort out the different effects of household characteristics and community involvement.

TESTING THE HYPOTHESES

We test these two proposed effects—community involvement and household composition—on census cooperation using the SIQSS monitoring data. We focus on the relationship between census cooperation and community involvement using a variety of civic engagement measures: length of time a person has lived in the same community, number of voluntary memberships, church attendance, and participation in different civic activities. Many of these measures are replicates of those used by Putnam (2000). We measure household composition with two variables: household type and the number of people in the household. Household type is a composite measure of different household characteristics, such as marital status, number of children below age eighteen in the household, and the total number of adults and children in the household. Using these original variables, we have created five indicators of the household type to capture the most common living arrangements found in the United States: (1) single respondents living alone; (2) single respondents living with adult roommates; (3) single respondents living with children under the age of eighteen; (4) married respondents without children in the household; and (5) married respondents with children in the household (the baseline in the multivariate model). Before turning to the multivariate analysis, we provide a descriptive look at the relationship between census cooperation and community involvement and household factors.

We first consider the relationship between community involvement and census cooperation. Table 4.1 reports the mail-back response rate of respondents by membership in various organizations.[5] For four organizations, members had higher census return rates than nonmembers. In two instances (school club or association and hobby, sports team, youth group), the data run in the opposite direction. Given the nature of those groups, we may be seeing a "school-age children" effect—parents with young children have busy lives and may forget to return their census form. The remaining six

Table 4.1   Group Membership, by Type and Census Cooperation

	Total Member-ship	Census Cooperation Among:		
		Members	Non-members	Difference
Service club or fraternity	14.1%	79.7%	81.0%	−1.1
Veterans' group	4.7	86.3	80.5	5.8
Religious group	32.4	83.6	79.4	4.2*
Senior citizens' center or group	6.2	92.9	79.9	13.0*
Women's group	8.4	88.2	80.1	8.1*
Labor union	7.2	74.7	81.2	−6.5
Issue-oriented political organization	4.3	87.6	80.4	7.2
Nonpartisan civic organization	4.7	85.8	80.5	5.3
School club or association	17.3	74.9	82.0	−7.1*
Hobby, sports team, youth group	34.5	76.2	83.2	−7.0*
Neighborhood or community association	17.0	88.5	79.1	9.4*
Group representing racial-ethnic interests	2.8	82.4	80.7	1.7

Source: Authors' compilation, SIQSS census baseline and follow-up survey, 2000, short form only.
Notes: N = 1,994. Two-tailed chi-square tests were used to determine significance of difference.
*p < .05

group types listed in table 4.1 show no significant differences between members and nonmembers in rates of census cooperation. Based on this initial look, then, the relationship between organizational membership and census cooperation is not entirely clear.

We next shift attention from organizational membership to a direct measure of civic involvement. Putnam (2000, 53) draws an appropriate distinction between membership in large mass organizations and active involvement in community activities. He notes that the former does not necessarily indicate the latter: the upward "trend in numbers of voluntary associations nationwide [is] not a reliable guide to trends in social capital, especially for associations that lack a structure of local chapters in which members can actually participate." In other words, writing a yearly check to the Sierra Club is not an appropriate measure of community involvement. Putnam focuses on membership in organizations that tend to involve active participation.

Table 4.2 reports census cooperation rates for activities that indicate "active involvement." Even with these more active measures, we find that

Table 4.2   Community Involvement and Census Cooperation

| | | Census Cooperation Among: | | |
Community Involvement	Total Involved	Involved	Non-Involved	Difference
Attended community group meeting	21.2%	85.1%	79.6%	5.5*
Worked for charity or church	34.2	84.8	78.6	6.2*
Worked with others in the community to solve a problem	18.1	84.2	80.0	4.2
Served on community board	5.3	82.0	80.7	1.3
Attended PTA or school group meeting	23.2	80.8	80.7	0.1
Donated blood	12.1	82.2	80.5	1.7
Gave money to charity	66.9	85.0	72.0	13.0*

Source: Authors' compilation, SIQSS census baseline and follow-up survey, 2000, short form only.
Notes: N = 1,994. Columns 2 and 3 give the percentage of respondents involved or not involved who mailed back the census (as a percentage of those respondents who received the short form and were part of the follow-up survey). Two-tailed chi-square tests were used to determine significance of difference.
*p < .05

only three of seven community involvement activities are associated with higher levels of census cooperation.[6]

Finally we consider respondents' length of residency in the community and levels of church attendance. We find that those who have been in the community for ten or more years cooperate with the census at higher rates than those who are comparatively newer to the community (table 4.3). The trend is less clear for church attendance but still suggests that those who never participate in religious activities return their census forms at a somewhat lower rate than those who are part of a church or religious community.

The bivariate patterns in the previous three tables suggest some association between community involvement and census cooperation, although the results are far from consistent. What about family characteristics? Table 4.4 shows bivariate relationships between census cooperation and two variables that measure household composition—household type and the number of people living in the household. Clearly, we can see that nontraditional family types, such as a household of adult roommates or a single person with kids, have the lowest census mail-back rate. Both married groups have relatively high return rates. Respondents who are married with children have a lower mail-back rate (83 percent) than those who are married without children (90 percent), suggesting that the time demands of child care work against taking on this particular civic duty. Larger households also have much lower mail-back rates than smaller households, perhaps because

Table 4.3   Census Mail-Back Rate, by Length in Community and Church Attendance

	Percentage of Respondents	Census Mail-Back Rate
Length in community		
Less than one year	8.3%	78.7%
One to ten years	50.8	77.7
More than ten years	40.9	85.1
Church attendance		
Never	23.1	77.8
Couple of times a year	30.9	82.1
Once or twice a month	8.1	76.4
Almost every week	10.5	84.6
Every week	27.4	83.5

Source: Authors' compilation, SIQSS census monitors and follow-up, March–June 2000.
Note: Valid N = 1,985 (length in community); 1,920 (church attendance).

Table 4.4   Census Mail-Back Rate, by Family Characteristics

	Percentage of Respondents	Census Mail-Back Rate
Household type		
Lives alone	14.0%	86%
Single with adult roommates	17.1	73
Single with kids	7.0	63
Married with no kids	44.0	90
Married with kids	17.9	83
Household size[a]		
One-person household	15.1	86
Two-persons household	44.1	88
Three-persons household	24.3	82
Four or more people	16.6	69

Source: Authors' compilation, SIQSS census baseline, monitors, and follow-up surveys.
Note: Valid N = 1,687.
[a]In multivariate analysis, household size is included as a continuous variable ranging from 1 to 8.

a census form is more difficult and time-consuming to fill out for larger households (and time may be more limited).

We next test the comparative influence of community involvement and household composition in the same multivariate model while controlling for other demographic factors associated with census cooperation. The results of the multivariate analyses are presented in table 4.5. The table reports the effects of civic engagement and household composition on census cooperation and voting while controlling for gender, age, education, race, employment, urbanicity, party identification, and political interest and knowledge (see table 4A.1 for full results).

First, we focus on the models predicting census cooperation (models 1 to 3). The results are presented in three stages. Model 1 tests the effect of the three measures of community involvement on census cooperation. Model 2 adds the number of civic activities to the model. This variable, which measures not just membership but active involvement in community groups (table 4.2), most closely matches Putnam's notion of social capital. Model 3 adds the household composition variables previously overlooked by much of the existing research on census cooperation.

The general finding is striking. With demographic and political characteristics controlled for, organizational membership and length of time in the community do not predict census behavior (model 1). Likewise,

Table 4.5   Logistic Regression Comparing Community and Family Effects on Census Cooperation and Voting

	Census Cooperation			Voted in 1996 Presidential Election		
	(1)	(2)	(3)	(4)	(5)	(6)
Community involvement						
Length in community[a]						
Less than one year	.088	.090	−.044	.116	.116	.132
More than ten years	.322[†]	.320[†]	.328[†]	.415***	.406***	.419***
Church attendance	.004	.004	.003	.007**	.005[†]	.004
Number of memberships	−.070	−.076	−.076	.123**	.024	.028
Number of civic activities		.015	.025		.230***	.213***
Household composition						
Household type[a]						
Lives alone			−.728*			−.378[†]
Single, adult roommates			−.705*			−.468**
Single with kids			−.926**			−.148
Married, no kids			.031			−.073
Household size			−.229**			−.043

Source: Models 1 to 3: Authors' compilation, SIQSS census follow-up survey, May–June 2000 (N = 1,570). Models 4 to 6: Authors' compilation, SIQSS census baseline survey, March 2000 (N = 3,880).

Notes: Cell entries are unstandardized coefficients from logistic regression. Models control for gender, age, education, race, employment, urbanicity, party identification, and political interest and knowledge. See table 4A.1 for full model.

[a]Compared to one to ten years in the same community and married with children under eighteen present in the household.

†p < .10; *p < .05; **p < .01; ***p < .001

adding in the number of civic activities (model 2)—a summary index of various ways in which the individual connects to his or her community—does not help us understand who will or will not return a census form. Except for a marginally significant positive effect of living in the neighborhood for more than ten years, none of the other community characteristics have a statistically significant effect on census participation.

In contrast, adding the household-type indicators and household size (model 3) finds many statistically significant relationships. In other words, understanding household composition helps us to predict the likelihood of census cooperation. Compared to the "traditional family" households in which respondents are married with children, the nontraditional family types are significantly less likely to return their census form. Single respondents with kids are the least likely to return their census form, but single respondents living with adult roommates and those living alone are also less likely to return their census form than those married with children. The insignificant coefficient for married couples without children shows that they have about the same likelihood of returning the census form as married couples with children (the baseline). The results also indicate, as expected, that as household size increases, the likelihood of returning the census decreases.

To compare the predictors of census cooperation and political participation, we replicate the model predicting census cooperation for voting turnout with voting in the presidential election in 1996 as the dependent variable (models 4 to 6 in table 4.5).[7] As previously discussed, it has been a long-running assumption that census participation and political participation are civic activities "cut from the same cloth."[8] Because we have found that community involvement variables do not in fact predict census cooperation as previously thought, we should confirm that these measures remain predictive of political participation. In other words, is community involvement a poor predictor of census participation only, or is it also inadequate to explain other forms of civic participation, namely voting behavior?

The findings for voter turnout confirm that community involvement still has a strong and positive effect on voting behavior. Model 4 shows that, controlling for demographic characteristics, those who have lived in the same community longer are more likely to have voted in 1996. Similarly, the more organizations an individual belongs to or the more often he or she attends church or other religious services, the more likely it is that he or she voted in 1996. Adding the number of civic activities to the model (model 5) washes out some of the effects of community involvement, but the clear result is that a community/civic engagement model has a significant positive effect on the likelihood of voting. In model 6, we find that household type is also an important predictor, but that the community involvement model still holds and the effects of household composition are not nearly as large as they are on census cooperation.

To better illustrate the substantive interpretation of these multivariate results, we use the fully specified models 3 and 6 from table 4.5 to calculate the predicted probability of voting and census cooperation across varying levels of civic participation and different household compositions.[9] Considering first how civic participation affects voting and census cooperation, figure 4.1 varies the number of civic activities for the average woman in a traditional family household. The solid line represents the predicted like-

Figure 4.1   Predicted Census Cooperation and Voting,
by Civic Participation

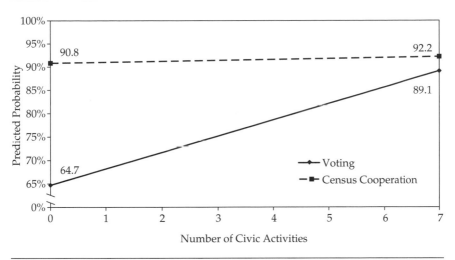

Source: Authors' compilation, SIQSS census monitors and follow-up, 2000.
Note: The effect of the number of civic activities on census cooperation is not statistically significant.

lihood of voting; the dotted line represents predicted census participation. The results are striking. An increasing number of civic activities, with all other variables held constant, increases the probability of voting from 65 to 89 percent. Each additional civic activity increases the likelihood of voting by three to four percentage points. In sharp contrast, the effect of civic activities on census behavior is minimal: these activities increase the probability of census cooperation by only one percentage point across the full range of civic activities (from 91 to 92 percent), a statistically insignificant increase. Respondents who are very civically active are more likely to vote, but not more likely to return a census form.[10]

We calculated similar scenarios for household composition variables. Figure 4.2 demonstrates the predicted probabilities of voting and census cooperation by household type. For voting, the differences between household types certainly exist but are relatively small. The voting rate is approximately the same for married couples with or without kids and for singles with kids (74, 72, and 71 percent, respectively). It is somewhat lower for those living alone (67 percent) and for singles living with adult roommates (64 percent). Although existing research on voting behavior has not explicitly explored a "household effect," these results are consistent

Figure 4.2   Predicted Census Cooperation and Voting,
              by Household Composition

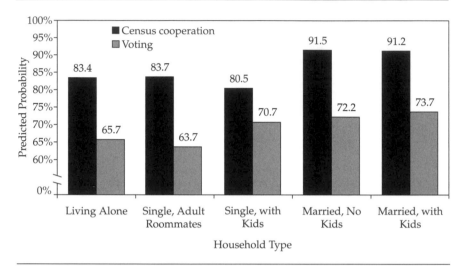

Source: Authors' compilation, SIQSS census baseline, monitors, and follow-up, 2000.
Notes: The presence of kids is measured as presence of household members below age
eighteen. Only living alone and living with adult roommates are significantly different
from married with kids for voting. All continuous variables are kept at mean and dichotomous ones at mode.

with long-standing findings that individuals who are younger and more
mobile and have fewer resources are less likely to vote.

In contrast, we find much sharper differences in census cooperation by
household type. Census cooperation rates are clearly higher for those who
are married (91 percent) than for respondents in nontraditional households.
Single respondents with kids have the lowest census mail-back rate (80 percent). Similarly, single respondents living with adult roommates have significantly lower census mail-back rate (84 percent). Unfortunately, our
typology of household types is not exhaustive. Ideally, we could separate
out, for instance, single adults who live in a marriagelike relationship from
those who live with roommates. We would expect that cooperation rates are
lower still for the latter group. Future research should look more closely at
other nontraditional living arrangements that are becoming increasingly
common: commuter marriages, group living quarters, and joint custody
households. Unfortunately, our measures do not allow us to completely sort
out the multiple and complicating ways in which the family as a social unit
interacts with the household, which is the unit that cooperates, or does not,
with the census. But the analysis here strongly suggests that family and

household type explains a significant amount of the variation in census cooperation. We conclude that the social capital generated by community involvement may provide the fuel for political participation, but not for census cooperation.

Robert Putnam showed his surprise over the Census Bureau's achievement of increasing the return rate in 2000 in an interview with the *New York Times*: "Against that background [overall decline in community involvement], to have successfully produced a two-percentage-point increase in mail-back response rates is actually stunning" (Holmes 2000). Our analysis suggests that Putnam is correct about the stunning achievement, but that he may have been focused on the wrong mountain the bureau had to climb. The trends in household composition will continue to present a daunting challenge to future census counts.

THE CHANGING AMERICAN HOUSEHOLD

It perhaps goes without saying that the typical American family is not what it used to be, whatever magical moment in the past one selects to embody such typicality. On dozens of different variables the picture of the American family has changed, sharply so, in the last three or four decades. One measure favored by social commentators is marital status; figure 4.3

Figure 4.3   Married Population in the United States, 1972 to 2000

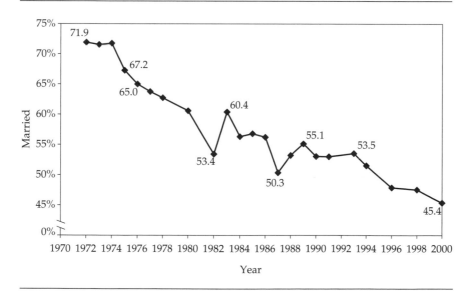

Source: General Social Survey, 1972 to 2000.

shows the steady decline in married adults, from 72 percent in 1972 to 45 percent in 2000.

More generally, between 1950 and 2000, married-couple households declined from more than three-fourths of all households (78 percent) to just over one-half (52 percent) (Hobbs and Stoops 2002). Similarly, the proportion of married-couple-with-children households has decreased. In 2000 fewer than half (46 percent) of married-couple households had a child under age eighteen, compared with 59 percent in 1960 (Hobbs and Stoops 2002). In the meantime, the percentage of one-parent family households with children under age eighteen doubled, from 4 percent in 1960 to 9 percent in 2000. The proportion of women in their twenties and thirties who have never married tripled between 1970 and 1992. Among twenty-five- to twenty-nine-year-old women, the percentage increased from 11 percent to 33 percent, and among thirty- to thirty-four-year-olds, from 6 percent to 19 percent (Saluter 1992). Finally, the number of unmarried-couple households was 4.7 million in 2000, or nine times the 1970 number.

The American family is also changing in ways other than marital status. The traditional multigenerational family is disappearing as children depart for college, working adults live in temporary company apartments away from the home, and the elderly move to retirement homes. The mean number of generations in a household declined from 1.62 in 1975 to 1.43 in 1998. And the percentage of households with a single occupant doubled between 1960 and 2000 (from 13 percent to 26 percent). The single-occupant household is the fastest-growing household type in the United States.

As family households have disappeared, nonfamily households have taken their place. Using Census Bureau criteria, the proportion of all nonfamily households was 19 percent in 1970 and increased to 33 percent in 2003. A steadily increasing number of people live with roommates, a trend that is especially common among young adults. Cutting across these changes in family composition are trends that redefine the household. College students are both at home and away, and they are numerous. For the affluent (family income above $80,000), college attendance rates increased from 70 percent in 1980 to 83 percent in 2000, and for the less affluent (family income below $33,000) from 40 percent to 60 percent in the same two decades. Commuter marriages are increasing as well, as is the number of people who move back and forth between two homes—second homes now number some 3.5 million. Our analysis suggests that these trends have profound implications for census-taking.

To reiterate the core finding in this chapter: the decline in community involvement, whatever it portends for social capital and political participation, cannot fully explain declines in census cooperation. There could be a sudden (and unexpected) reversal of the community involvement and civic engagement trends at the center of Putnam's analysis, but we would not anticipate a corresponding increase in census cooperation. Instead, our analysis suggests that basic household structure and composition have a much stronger impact on census cooperation. The deep social-demographic changes in the family structure and residency patterns in the United States of the last few decades have affected census participation, making it increasingly difficult to sustain reasonable levels of census cooperation. Mobilization messages that promote census participation as a family activity will become less and less appropriate in the effort to maintain census mail-back cooperation. Despite the inevitable and enormous complications, our analysis suggests that it might be necessary to reconsider the basic household-centered design on which the U.S. census has always been based.

Table 4A.1   Community and Family Effects on Voting and Census Cooperation: Full Models

	Census Cooperation			Vote in 1996		
	(1)	(2)	(3)	(1)	(2)	(3)
Control variables						
Female	.491**	.487**	.514**	.414***	.365***	.387***
Age	.100***	.099***	.055*	.109***	.097***	.083***
Age squared	-.001**	-.001**	.000	-.001***	-.001**	.000*
Years of education	.074†	.073†	.057	.172***	.160***	.161***
African American	-.730**	-.726**	-.597*	.002	.043	.089
Hispanic	-.105	-.105	.030	-.309†	-.279†	-.285†
Asian American	-.456	-.456	-.604	-1.723***	-1.728***	-1.778***
Working	.235	.231	.261	.525***	.487***	.493***
Rural[a]	-.576**	-.576**	-.563**	-.184	-.209†	-.187
Central city[a]	.030	.031	.070	-.170†	-.156	-.129
Republican	.175	.174	.115	1.042***	1.039***	1.036***
Democrat	.521**	.521**	.526**	.998***	.997***	1.008***
Interest in politics	.398	.390	.411	1.551***	1.460***	1.465***
Political knowledge	-.024	-.031	-.031	1.111***	1.048***	1.035***
Community involvement						
Length in community[a]						
Less than one year	.088	.090	-.044	.116	.116	.132
More than ten years	.322†	.320†	.328†	.415***	.406***	.419***
Church attendance	.004	.004	.003	.007**	.005†	.004
Number of memberships	-.070	-.076	-.076	.123**	.024	.028

	(1)	(2)	(3)	(4)	(5)	(6)
Number of civic activities		.015	.025		.230***	.213***
Family composition						
Household type[a]						
Lives alone			-.728*			-.378†
Single, adult roommates			-.705*			-.468**
Single, with kids			-.926**			-.148
Married, no kids			.031			-.073
Household size			-.229**			-.043
Constant	-2.775***	-2.748***	-.466	-7.552***	-7.229***	-6.622***
Model chi-square	125.1***	125.1***	156.3***	1284.5***	1311.3***	1323.4***
Degrees of freedom	18	19	24	18	19	24
Change in chi-square	4.9	.04	31.2***	46.1***	26.8***	12.1*
Degrees of freedom	4	1	5	4	1	5
Nagelkerke R^2	.14	.14	.17	.42	.43	.43
Valid N	1,570	1,570	1,570	3,880	3,880	3,880

Source: Authors' compilation, SIQSS census baseline, monitors, and follow-up surveys.

Notes: Cell entries are unstandardized coefficients from logistic regression.

[a]Compared to medium urban areas, one to ten years in the same community, and married with children under eighteen present in the household.

†p < .10; *p < .05; **p < .01; ***p < .00

Chapter Five | Conclusions and Consequences

EVERY DECENNIAL CENSUS differs in design and methodology from the one that preceded it.[1] Our inquiry started by setting out the context for the 2000 census because every census is responsive to the inevitable changes in the social-political climate and the demographic context over the ten-year interval. Census design also changes because every census offers lessons for how to do the next one. Although the Census Bureau conducts a "test census" during the planning phase of every census, this is a weak substitute for the real thing—much as the Pentagon's "war games" are a weak substitute for the real thing. Because the decennial is a learning opportunity for the Census Bureau, an extensive evaluation program is imbedded in each decennial on the basis of which the next census is shaped.

It is in this spirit that we ask how our findings might be valuable in designing the 2010 census. The challenge of translating social science findings into policy recommendations has been a continuing theme for well over a century, dating to the nineteenth-century origins of the academic disciplines as we know them today. This discussion has often been framed as if there is a clear distinction between "basic" and "applied" social science, a distinction we find useless. Here we discard it in favor of a distinction between social science knowledge and policy knowledge. Metaphors are risky, but we might liken social science knowledge to an aquifer and policy knowledge as the ability to drill into that resource pool in a manner that facilitates making, defending, and changing policy. Social science knowledge tells us what is there—in our study, for example, it showed us how a civic mobilization campaign worked and how privacy concerns compromised that campaign. Policy knowledge tells us how to use these findings *in real-world contexts*. It requires going beyond the empirical findings to take into account known constraints and probable developments. Policy knowledge, so defined, blends social science findings with

114

sensitivity to what is reasonable to expect under current resource and policy conditions.

Bearing this in mind, we start with the key findings in each of our three empirical chapters:

1. The mobilization campaign in 2000 was effective in improving the mail-back cooperation rate above what had been predicted, and it was particularly effective in reaching the population groups that are most often undercounted.

2. Privacy and confidentiality concerns depress cooperation with the census and, if inflamed during the census itself, as they were in 2000, compromise census coverage and increase selectivity in answering questions (item nonresponse), leading to a deterioration of data quality.

3. Household structure and composition, especially in light of rapid changes over the last few decades in the household composition of traditional and nontraditional families in the United States, influence census cooperation in ways that call into question the household as the appropriate unit of data collection and data reporting.

Although our focus is on the decennial census, each of these findings has implications for the survey-based information system on which our government (and economy) depend. There are approximately seventy federal statistical programs and agencies that operate at a total annual budget of $5 billion and generate a steady flow of statistics about the nation's population and economic establishments. In the end, the resulting national statistical system is based on millions upon millions of citizens *voluntarily* checking boxes, completing forms, and answering questions. Anything that erodes this compliance compromises the quality of the nation's statistics—and of course, the policy and economic decisions based on them.

In thinking about how the 2000 census experience can inform future censuses, we must recognize that the 2010 census is expected to be fundamentally changed by the American Community Survey (ACS), a major innovation now under way. If the ACS is fully implemented, the 2010 census will not include a long form. So, before drawing out the implications of what we have learned about public cooperation with the government's statistical data collection, we briefly introduce the American Community Survey.

THE AMERICAN COMMUNITY SURVEY

The ACS is a large, continuous sample survey designed to replace the decennial census long form. It is administered to approximately three million households each year, and this summary provides yearly estimates of population and household characteristics for communities of 65,000 or larger. To make the results of the ACS available at the smaller levels of geography provided by current long-form data, the survey combines multiple-year data. After the ACS has been in the field for five years its sample will be fifteen million addresses, somewhat less than the nineteen million for the decennial long form in 2000. Higher response rates and more complete questionnaires help to offset the impact of the smaller sample. When fully implemented the ACS will use three-year averages to provide estimates for populations as small as 20,000, and five-year averages to provide estimates down to the census tract (average of 4,000 persons) and block group level (average of 1,500 persons). Five years of data, then, offer geographic detail comparable to what is now available from the long form. Because the ACS will be fielded every year, each measure is updated annually rather than on decadal basis.[2]

This annual survey will also answer the main criticism of the decennial long form—that it produces stale information. With the long form, administered only every ten years, a community or business must make do with information that grows increasingly out-of-date until the next decennial refreshes it. It is this fundamental deficiency in the long-form design that the ACS corrects. Annually updated information on the population and household characteristics that appear in the long-form data is an enormous step forward in census-taking.

This is not the place for detailed review of the ACS; extensive documentation can be found on the Census Bureau website. Following years of testing, the ACS was implemented in 2005; and, as of this writing (November 2005) it is expected to receive budget authorization for 2006. Although an expensive undertaking, with annual costs approximating $150 million, this investment will be recouped by having a much less costly decennial census in 2010 and beyond. Congress agrees that cost-benefit calculations work strongly in favor of the ACS. Of course congressional appropriations are unpredictable, but knowledgeable observers believe that if the ACS is adequately funded in FY06 and FY07, it will develop a strong constituency of users. The 2010 census will, then, be a short-form-only census, and it is on this assumption that our discussion proceeds.

A SHORT-FORM-ONLY CENSUS

The constitutional purpose of the decennial census is to count and geographically locate the population. Supreme Court cases require that this be done with precision for small geographic areas so as to ensure that congressional and other electoral districts are as close to equal in size as is feasible. Drawing the lines of electoral districts to reflect the distribution of the eighteen-and-over population can come down to deciding on the placement of geographical units as small as a block. The Voting Rights Act complicates this process because under its provisions electoral boundaries have to be drawn in a way that does not put candidates supported by racial minorities at a disadvantage.

Viewing these constitutional and statutory requirements from the perspective of the census helps us see what questions the short form must include. The census information necessary to meet the legal requirements of reapportionment and redistricting must include, at a minimum: (1) an address for purposes of geographic location; (2) a household count by age; and (3) race and ethnicity to meet the requirements of the Voting Rights Act. Age is heavily used in the redistricting process—to identify the voting-age population—and is not likely to leave the short form. Other items, such as proper names and gender, are used by the bureau in quality control procedures, especially to assist in finding duplicates in the census.

In this chapter, we consider how lessons from the 2000 census could be carried into the design of a short-form-only census for 2010. In turn, we analyze the policy consequences of each of the key aspects of our analysis of the 2000 census: the mobilization efforts, the privacy debate, and household composition trends.

CIVIC MOBILIZATION

If the primary goals of the 2010 census remain focused, as they should, on a high mail-back rate and a low differential undercount, then our analysis suggests that it will be important to sustain a major outreach effort, including both the partnership program and a targeted paid-advertising campaign.

Although the differential undercount was substantially reduced in 2000, it would be imprudent to declare that the issue has been resolved or that the undercount has reached acceptable levels. As we have previously noted, the 2000 census was unusually well funded. The conditions behind the generous funding, including a robust economy and an unprecedented partisan dynamic, are unlikely to be duplicated in 2010 (Prewitt 2003/2005, 36–37). Reduced funding, particularly the underfunding of a promotional campaign such as that used in 2000, is likely to lead to a higher differential undercount in 2010. Insofar as maintaining a low differential undercount remains a central concern in census planning, our findings suggest that the payoff lies in a mobilization effort targeted to population groups that are typically less likely to participate in the census.

A short-form-only census, however, will require a subtle change in the message content. In 2000, the central mobilization message was: "This [an illustration of the census form] is your future. Don't leave it blank." The future was portrayed as less crowded schools, improved social services, and fairer distribution of federal funds. Promotional material emphasized that one's community would benefit from a more complete count, with "community" sometimes specified as the neighborhood and sometimes as a racial or ethnic community. Although not directly emphasized, these community benefits in large part stem from information provided in the census long form. The message could still work for a short-form-only census, though it should probably be modified to indicate more strongly the link between simple population numbers and federal funding formulas.

Since there will be less need to motivate long-form cooperation, it will also be possible to have the mobilization campaign in 2010 focus on the connection between population numbers and political representation. In doing so, the campaign can help to increase public understanding of how our democracy works, not an insignificant side benefit. Currently, the direct link from population distribution to redistricting to elections to public policy is not well understood by the general public. Thus, a mobilization campaign of the scope used in 2000 could not only sustain a high level of census cooperation but provide a civics lesson on the numerical underpinnings of representative democracy.

This shift in emphasis is more likely to occur if the census is viewed as what in fact it is: the *nonpartisan* starting point of *partisan* political representation. Whether 2010 will be the first census in thirty years to unfold free of partisan bickering is uncertain, but it seems unlikely that the design itself will be as politicized as it was in 2000.[3] If we make this assumption and further assume that political leaders will not tell citizens that the census is intrusive, a fully bipartisan engagement with the mobilization effort could sustain cooperation and advance the constitutionally derived civics lesson that underpins the census in the first place.

More ambitiously, a short-form-only census should be designed as a civic ceremony—imagine 535 members of Congress completing their census form at the Jefferson Memorial on Census Day. The census is in fact the only such civic ceremony available to American political life. It is inclusive, it is nonpartisan, and it is consequential. July 4 no longer has this character, nor, except for veterans, does Armistice Day. Presidents' Day in February is a shopping spree. The 9/11 anniversary is on its way to being commercialized, if it has not already been politicized. And in the key moments in the presidential cycle—the swearing-in ceremony, the State of the Union address—partisanship has trumped any civic message.

To some extent, our data suggest that a civic mobilization message might provide a less compelling motive to participate than a "material benefits" message. But portraying the census as a civic ceremony would come quite naturally if it had bipartisan support. If both political parties can offer unconditional support for the short-form-only census, then it will be much easier to develop a dual message that emphasizes civic and legal responsibility while at the same time highlighting the individual material incentives of federal funding and political representation. There is already public recognition that census cooperation is a civic obligation. Nearly three of every five Americans agree that "it is our civic responsibility to fill out the census," and more than half (56 percent) already recognize that Congress is reapportioned on the basis of the census numbers. There is a base on which to build a stronger civics lesson into the census promotion. This will be both more relevant and easier to accomplish in a short-form-only census. The constitutional reason for the decennial census can be emphasized once it is no longer necessary to motivate millions of households to complete the long form.

There is another, more fundamental motivation for using the census to promote a civics lesson. In a democracy, statistical information is a public good. This public good is particularly vulnerable to collective action problems because it exists only if high levels of cooperation are reached. An election works even if only half of the population votes; its outcome still determines who has the constitutional right to govern the country. In contrast, if only half the population completes a census form, the information loses its utility. Likewise, a 50 percent cooperation rate with the Current Population Survey or American Community Survey or any of dozens of critical sample-based federal surveys puts our national statistical system at serious risk. The stakes riding on public support for and cooperation with the national statistical system become clearer as we consider the second finding on census cooperation and privacy concerns.

PRIVACY AND CONFIDENTIALITY

In many respects, the interaction of privacy concerns with census-taking is nothing new. President Washington was referring to privacy when he noted that the "scruples" of some led to uncooperativeness with the nation's first census. More recently, other nations have experienced privacy revolts with consequences more far-reaching than what we have discussed for the U.S. census. A 1980s study found that privacy and confidentiality issues were prominent in six countries: the Netherlands, the United Kingdom, Australia, New Zealand, Canada, and Germany (Mayer 2002). In some instances, notably the Netherlands and Germany, widespread protests about the lack of privacy protection and potential data misuse ultimately led to changes in how those countries collect population information.

The Netherlands case is instructive. In its 1960 census, the government recorded almost no cases of refusal to cooperate. The turbulent 1960s changed this, and refusal rates climbed sharply in the 1971 census even though the census had already been delayed for a year in order to strengthen the law protecting Dutch citizens against privacy violations (Laan 2000). The stronger law notwithstanding, about 2 percent of the population refused to cooperate. As the Netherlands prepared for its 1981 census, surveys found that the refusal rate could increase to one-quarter of the population, with rates as high as 60 percent in urban areas. Obviously, at those levels the census would be useless. The Netherlands postponed and then canceled the census altogether when the Dutch Parliament voted to discontinue the traditional enumeration-based census. It was replaced with a design that combines administrative information with continuous labor force sample surveys and a housing demographic sample survey taken on a four-year cycle (Stadt and Vliegen 1992; Vliegen and Stadt 1988).

Germany had a similar experience. As it prepared for its scheduled 1981 census, advocacy groups initiated a campaign focused on confidentiality violation issues, alleging that the census data would be used for something other than strictly statistical purposes. The Constitutional Court ruled that it was a violation of an individual's right to privacy to use census data to update population registers and, further, that citizens could refuse to answer sensitive census questions, including place of employment, number of automobiles, health status, and income. This did not placate opponents of the census, and Germany's 1981 decennial census was postponed. In early 1983 the Constitutional Court suspended the census altogether pending stronger confidentiality protections in data dissemination procedures (Butz and Scarr 1987). More than two years later legislation detailed acceptable content, field procedures, and data release provisions. The census was finally carried out in 1987, six years after its initial scheduled date, and even then not without strong opposition from privacy advocacy groups, which widely distributed anticensus material urging noncooperation (Butz and Scarr 1987; Choldin 1988). Responding in large part to these privacy concerns, the German decennial census has now been replaced with a microcensus that directly enumerates just 1 percent of the total population, with additional data provided by supplementary surveys.

The Dutch and German cases show that acceptable levels of cooperation with a national census can evaporate quickly. In those instances cooperation deteriorated so quickly that from one decennial to the next each of these countries decided to terminate census-taking as the central element in its national statistical system.

PRIVACY AND FUTURE U.S. CENSUS COUNTS

How possible is it that the United States will follow in the tracks of Germany and the Netherlands? We address this question through the filter of a decennial census in which the long form has migrated to the American Community

Survey. The obvious and most important observation is that a loud, nation-wide privacy debate over the short form *cannot* get the traction that the privacy debate did in 2000, which was almost exclusively focused on long-form questions. What moves to the fore in a short-form-only census design is that the country must have this count to fulfill the constitutional mandate to realign political representation with population growth. Even the critics who in 2000 were most outraged and who labeled the census as intrusive were quick to emphasize that they would answer those questions necessary to obtain the basic household count.

But if a short-form-only decennial census is less vulnerable, other government surveys—especially the very large ACS—will be subject to privacy concerns. Individual members of Congress will hear (and in scattered cases, already have heard) from constituents who find the ACS questions intrusive. This experience is far different in impact, however, from that of nearly 17 million households getting the long form in the span of a few days during which a media campaign is drawing attention to the census. In the ACS it takes five years or more before this many households are asked the long-form questions, and they are approached one household at a time rather than in the midst of a nationally visible campaign.

To note that a short-form-only census is largely immunized from the sharp and sudden public outcry that occurred in 2000 is not to say that privacy concerns will be inconsequential. Even scattered complaints to enough individual members of Congress can have an effect on how hard the Census Bureau pushes to get complete coverage. Moreover, public cooperation with the decennial census, the ACS, and hundreds of other government surveys will continue to be affected by the steadily growing proportion of the public fearing breaches of confidentiality and resisting the intrusiveness of survey questions. And though the ACS will be insulated from concentrated media attention on its "intrusiveness," it will also not benefit from a concurrent, broad, national mobilization campaign designed to increase census cooperation, as occurs during the decennial. Because the U.S. government cannot fund a massive media campaign before each of its important surveys, it becomes even more important to create general public support for the national statistical system.

In chapter 3, we discussed the conceptual distinction between confidentiality and privacy, describing the former as protection against disclosure of survey responses and the latter as protection from unwanted intrusiveness. To both of these public concerns the Census Bureau has for decades offered the same answer: "Don't be concerned, your answers are safe with us." This confidentiality promise is backed by law and policy, as well as firewalls and other disclosure avoidance procedures. The Census Bureau has long operated with an exceptionally strong law guaranteeing that answers to its surveys are to be used for statistical purposes only. This guarantee now extends to all government statistics. The Confidential Information Protection and Statistical Efficiency Act of 2002 (CIPSEA) prohibits the release of any information collected by a federal statistical agency for statistical purposes from being disclosed in an identifiable form for nonstatistical purposes. (For more detailed discussion, see National Research Council 2005.)

This government-wide policy is critically important in an era when many Americans believe that answers they give to the government or to their hospital, bank, and local supermarket are likely to be disclosed without their consent or knowledge. The census and government surveys have to contend with the serious collateral damage that occurs when, for instance, the Social Security Administration reveals an ad hoc policy of cooperation with the Department of Homeland Security, or a huge store of digitized credit card records go missing from a commercial site. Already, as noted earlier, approximately two of five Americans do not believe the Census Bureau's pledge of confidentiality. This number is likely to grow. Strong laws, policies, and practices are the best answer to these worrisome levels of public disbelief about inappropriate disclosure by the government. Our analysis also highlights the importance of communicating these policies to the public, especially when they are being asked to provide extensive personal information to the government.

Even if 100 percent of the public believe in the security of their answers to the census, a number—probably a growing number—will refuse to answer questions they view as intrusive. When President Bush said in 2000 that if he got the long form he was not sure he would answer all the questions, it was not fear of disclosure that he had in mind but government intrusiveness.

A pledge of confidentiality will not sate those who refuse to cooperate because they perceive the census as a violation of privacy. The government's statistical programs are now confronting the problem that public reaction to "intrusiveness" calls for a different strategy than public reaction to fears of disclosure, leading the Census Bureau to consider a new "principle of privacy." This principle suggests that, for voluntary surveys, the bureau "will respect the respondent's right to refuse to answer any questions" and "will set reasonable limits on the number of follow-up contacts." This represents a shift in tone at the bureau: historically it has respected the individual respondent but also been aggressive in maintaining high response rates and getting complete information. If the bureau becomes less insistent when respondents say, "Leave me alone, I don't want to be bothered," the resulting incomplete coverage and incomplete information will weaken data quality.

Because the new principle of privacy applies only to voluntary surveys, it excludes the decennial census and the American Community Survey, which remain mandatory. It is nevertheless a delicate dance to tell the public that, on the one hand, "your right to privacy is respected and we won't push too hard," and that, on the other, "the government wants this information and you have to give it."

Promising confidentiality and treating the respondent with respect are, finally, weak responses to growing resistance to government questions considered intrusive. What else is available? Using improved statistical techniques to compensate for nonresponse and missing data is a possibility, but to do so is also to accept declining cooperation rates. At some point, of course, statistical techniques, such as imputation, are no longer an option. Imputation fails if those who refuse to answer survey questions are sufficiently different from those who provide answers because the latter respondents are used to estimate characteristics of the former. And the absolute magnitude of nonresponse can become too high to trust imputation rates. In 2000, the 32 percent nonresponse on the property tax item was thought by some in the Census Bureau to have reached that limit, and the bureau seriously reviewed whether to report data that were one-third imputed. In fact, the Office of Management and Budget's statistical policy office has a directive requiring that a special bias estimation be applied if item nonresponse exceeds 30 percent for information in a government report.

Of course, the government could also deal with declining cooperation rates by shifting from a full population enumeration to a design that combines a more extensive use of administrative data with a sample survey, as Germany and the Netherlands have done. For the U.S. decennial census, this would require two unlikely developments: first, a statutory change, or Supreme Court interpretation of the census statute, that reversed the 1999 decision prohibiting statistical sampling in constructing the apportionment count; and second, some type of national registry system linked to addresses that could provide the appropriate sampling frame.

At present, there are only two population groups for which registration is mandatory: males eligible for military service and non-nationalized immigrants. This is far different from the Netherlands, Germany, and many other European societies where all residents register in the local community as soon as they establish a domicile. In the United States, with its unwieldy arrangements for linking individuals to addresses, arrangements that are variable across municipal, county, and state governments, there are substantial administrative challenges to the establishment of a residency-based national registry. There is also citizen fear of state power and a corresponding resistance to what many will view as infringement on individual liberties.[4]

Of course even if these administrative and political barriers could be overcome, there is still the substantial task of linking residency files to other governmental data (let alone commercial data) that might provide a substitute to long-form data. The Census Bureau has in fact explored whether administrative data could be used to supplement census nonresponse. A 1995 Census Test attempted to match actual census records with information from more than forty commercial, federal, state, and local administrative databases in three different regions of the country. These data records were then matched with actual test census results. Less than 25 percent of census households could be completely matched to administrative record households (Leggieri and Killion 2000).

The Census Bureau conducted a similar experiment in 2000 to evaluate the feasibility of conducting an administrative records census or using administrative records to substitute for non-responding households. The Administrative Records Experiment 2000 found that although 81 percent of households from the administrative records could be linked to census households, just 51 percent of those matched households showed the same household size (Bauder and Judson 2003). Among the nonresponse households, the data quality was much worse. Just 62 percent of imputed households could be matched to administrative records, and of those matched, just 23 percent showed the same demographic composition in both the census and administrative records (Bauder and Judson 2003). Thus, the existing research attempting to match administrative and census records raises significant concerns about the quality and accuracy of an administrative census (Bauder and Judson 2003; Zanutto and Zaslavsky 2002).

If the decennial itself is unlikely to be replaced with a design that draws heavily on administrative data, the government's information system more generally will move in that direction if the standard methods fail. Government surveys will increasingly encounter a public saying, "Leave me alone," and solutions to noncompliance will be costly. Since the government will not forgo population information, it will probably search for alternatives that use huge amounts of already collected administrative data, and it seems reasonable to predict that it may begin to incorporate commercially collected digital information. Consider the 2000 long-form questions. Does the census have to ask an income question if the Internal Revenue Service (IRS) already has that information? Why ask about home mortgages if a bank or credit service can supply that information? Why include a question about distance driven to work if the government can easily link home address, place of employment, and EasyPass records? The vast amount of data pouring into various digital systems, the powerful data-mining algorithms available, and the new high-tech data collection possibilities (for example, transponders to measure travel patterns) have created a virtual "digital person" of each of us.

A national statistical system that makes greater use of administrative and commercial data is worrisome. It can too easily breach the historic firewall between administrative and statistical data. Linking the two information sources places at risk the protections historically associated with statistical information, which have ensured that survey responses can never be used against a respondent. Administrative data, unlike statistical data, draw attention to specific individuals, and this is the basis on which the records are stored. Commercial data have a different problem. There are few controls over what is collected, how it is collected, or how it is used. The public can refuse "intrusive" government questions; it cannot so easily say "leave me alone" to the conveniences of a digitized economy.

And of course, there are largely unexamined data quality issues. For decades scholars have steadily improved survey data—from sampling theory to questionnaire wording—and the federal statistical system, and thus the country, has been a major beneficiary. No comparable effort has been mounted with respect to highly error-prone administrative data. Quality control in commercial information is taken even less seriously. Commercial sites are not likely to welcome debates on quality of data arising from errors of commission and omission.

Ironically, if the American public, worried about privacy and confidentiality, withdraws its voluntary cooperation with the census and government surveys, it will hasten the development of an error-prone information system over which there are fewer controls on disclosure and even less personal privacy.

To prevent this, it will be necessary for the government to mount an even more aggressive public education campaign than the one pursued in 2000. The public will have to come to understand that official statistical information is a public good that requires setting aside resistance to what in 2000 were labeled intrusive questions. Of course, such an educational campaign can be mounted only if it is bipartisan.

The results of our analysis offer promise that a public education campaign can make headway, especially in the context of a decennial census that has the entire population as its audience. The census is perhaps the government's only opportunity to broadcast widely a message about the role of information in democratic policymaking and the vulnerability of that information to noncompliance. Bipartisan agreement on such a message is essential to deterring or at least minimizing potential damage by the media, political pundits, and late night comics.

FAMILY AND HOUSEHOLD COMPOSITION

The third consequential finding from our study is, unfortunately, the one least developed. It unfolded in two stages. First, the result on which the most confidence can be placed is the finding that community involvement factors are much less predictive of census cooperation than had been generally assumed by both scholars and the Census Bureau itself. Second, there appears to be a relationship between census cooperation and household composition, and here the characteristics predictive of cooperation are in sharp decline. Our analysis indicates that traditional households are much more likely to return their census form than nontraditional households. Households composed of a married couple (with or without children) return forms at higher rates than households composed of roommates, single parents, or a lone resident. Although our data cannot sort out the causal mechanisms between household composition and census cooperation, this is an important and previously overlooked relationship.

Our analysis suggests that family factors intertwine with, but are not identical to, major changes in household composition, especially in the growing numbers of unrelated people sharing living quarters, the growing number of commuter relations and joint custody arrangements, and the growing number of single-person households. Associated with these changes in family patterns and household living arrangements are problems with the Census Bureau's residency rules. These rules date to 1790; though modified many times since, they are not equipped to handle a number of current conditions, such as the dual residencies maintained by "snowbirds" or by those who move back and forth between a city apartment and a weekend home. The Census Bureau is conducting a major review of its residency rules, but even after correcting for current ambiguities, the complications associated with changes in family patterns and household living arrangements will remain.

The difficulties that complicated living arrangements create for census-taking can be illustrated with a hypothetical family of four from San Francisco. In this hypothetical family, the youngest child is studying at Santa Clara University, only twenty-five miles away. She lives with three roommates in a university apartment but returns to her San Francisco home every Wednesday (when she has no classes), every weekend, and every vacation break, thus spending approximately half her time in San Francisco. One reason the daughter goes home so often is to be company for her father, whose wife, a corporate consultant, travels weekly to Phoenix, where she stays in a company-provided apartment for three or four days each week. The older child, a recent college graduate, is taking some time off and working as a ski instructor in Lake Tahoe; he lives in a family-owned ski cabin in Truckee.

This family appears four times in the master address file of the Census Bureau: at the San Francisco home, at the university apartment, at the Phoenix apartment, and at the Truckee cabin. It is possible, then, that this family will return four census forms. The father may complete the form for the San Francisco address on the assumption that the household includes four members because the children are frequently there and are living off his income. His wife does not return the form that appeared in her Phoenix mailbox, which she seldom opens because email is her primary mail system. And the apartment has no phone number because she uses only a cell phone. But a census enumerator later records her at the Phoenix address, using information supplied by the apartment building doorman, who confirmed that she was there "most of the time." Meanwhile, the daughter has been listed, without her knowledge, on a census form completed (correctly) by a roommate. And the son, unsure what to do, decides to return the form mailed to the Truckee address, just in case. A number of other response combinations are possible, depending on who is interpreting the census residency rules and how carefully.

Although improved residency rules could reduce the ambiguities in this hypothetical case, the uncertainties and data instabilities associated with the family/household as the primary unit of data collection will remain in census-taking. If our finding about a family effect holds up under more detailed analysis, it suggests a major new challenge in the ongoing task of sustaining high levels of cooperation in a mail-back census.

The most dramatic way to pose this challenge is to ask whether the practice of using the household as the primary unit of data collection and reporting should be seriously reengineered, allowing for a design that in some circumstances would keep the household as the primary unit but under other circumstances would shift to the individual. For example, might it be preferable for unrelated persons sharing living quarters (though not inhabiting what the Census Bureau terms "group quarters") to be counted as individuals rather than as household members?

To take an extreme example,[5] there is really no average household income for the four roommates in the Santa Clara University apartment, but had that address received a long form in 2000, the census assumption would have been that it had a household income. Similarly, if the (hypothetical) Phoenix and Truckee addresses, with, respectively, a part-time resident and a seasonal resident, had received a census long form that was not returned, it is likely that both households would have received imputed values for household income. And for the ski instructor living in the family home, that imputed income would no doubt be far from the actual value.

We offer this example not, of course, to engage the enormously complicated issues of family structure, household composition, and residency rules or to pronounce on how the census might be redesigned for the twenty-first century. Our analysis very clearly suggests that these issues need careful consideration, but our study was focused on a much simpler

question about the conditions that explain overall levels of census cooperation. On that simpler question we offer an observation. From the perspective of our research, census cooperation—or at least, the mail-back response
rate—can decline for reasons unrelated to those previously assumed, most
often a decline in community ties. It may decline for reasons more closely
linked to changes in family and household structures. This finding should
be taken into account as the Census Bureau designs programs for future
censuses that encourage census cooperation by putting less emphasis on
"community benefit" and family-centered themes and more emphasis on
the responsibility of all individuals to ensure that they are included.

CONCLUSIONS

Census 2000 had its surprises, as does the story line unfolding as a result
of our study. We started with the obvious question: given the decline in
levels of census cooperation, could the unprecedented mobilization and
outreach effort planned for 2000 ensure that the Census Bureau reached its
target of a 61 percent mail-back rate? The first surprise, of course, was that
the target was not only met but substantially bettered. The final rate even
improved on the 1990 level. We have documented how this happened, giv-
ing particular attention to the success of the campaign focused on hard-to-
locate and hard-to-count residents, whose proportion of the population
had increased between 1990 and 2000. The consequences of this achievement reached well beyond confirming the wisdom of a congressional decision to fund the census mobilization program and well beyond awarding
boasting rights to the bureau and its partners and contractors. The achievement made for a less expensive census than anticipated.[6] More importantly,
it contributed to a higher-quality census than expected, especially insofar as
it reduced the differential undercount that has shadowed census-taking
for more than a half-century.

As is made clear by our data and by the sharp increase in the differential rate at which the census short form and long form were returned, this
achievement would have been greater yet had privacy issues not been
inflamed during the critical weeks in which the census forms were to be
returned. That the American public has privacy and confidentiality concerns about the government is not a surprise; nor should we be surprised
that these concerns surface during census-taking. Not expected, however,
was the strength with which the concerns were voiced and the partisan politics in which they became enmeshed. Although it is unlikely that 2010 will
be a repeat of 2000, privacy and confidentiality issues are bound to remain
a factor in the 2010 census and in government surveys more generally.
They will also affect levels of cooperation, even if the census is reduced to

the minimal information required to update the reapportionment and redistricting numbers and enforce the Voting Rights Act (which may in any case be altered prior to 2010). If, as is possible, the nation considers some form of a "national registration system" between now and 2010, and if the public comes to see the decennial census as part of such a system, there will no doubt be consequences for census cooperation. Too many contingencies preclude a reasoned prediction on such matters, but for the indefinite future census planning should assume that confidentiality fears ("I worry that my answers will be shared") and privacy concerns ("The government has no right to know that about me") are a permanent part of our public culture.

The research result that most surprised us was a negative finding—the absence of a relationship between levels of community involvement and census cooperation. The negative finding is paired with a positive finding that is equally surprising, the indication that there may be a household-based model that better predicts census cooperation than the community-based model. We have emphasized, and do so again, that in our data the specification of a household-based model is too incomplete to do more than hint at what might be there. But the hint is tantalizing, because it makes intuitive sense when combined with trends that point to an increasing divergence between traditional family structure and the actual living arrangements in millions of American households. The practical implications of this for census-taking are enormous and point, we believe, to a time when the household as historically conceptualized may no longer work as the primary unit of data collection and data reporting.

It is beyond the scope of this study to ask how the transition away from the household unit might be managed, or what might replace it. Our concern has been to understand how Census 2000 achieved unexpectedly high levels of census cooperation, as well as to uncover the factors that still kept cooperation at less than optimal levels (a 100 percent mail-back return rate, of course). In addition to the attitudinal and demographic factors analyzed throughout, we report that privacy concerns have depressed cooperation, that they are likely to continue to do so, and that a complicated dynamic in household composition may turn out to be even more consequential for the quality of the decennial census in the nation's future.

Our findings point to a question that reaches beyond the decennial census: how will the national statistical system evolve over the next several decades? It is already clear that a significant number of citizens no longer trust the government's promise of confidentiality regarding their survey responses. In addition, more and more citizens, urged on by political leaders with a libertarian bent, are saying, "Leave me alone. Stop asking your intrusive questions." Consequently, voluntary compliance with data collection efforts is bound to erode, for all of the reasons highlighted throughout the book. The census in 2000 may, in retrospect, come to be seen as a turning point—the time when the nation's information system began to move away from its reliance on sample survey data to one that relies more on administratively collected data as well as commercially collected digital information—much of the latter from surveillance over which we have little control. Such a "system," if that is the right word to use, brings to our democratic politics a raft of new privacy, confidentiality, transparency, and data quality concerns.

Throughout the twentieth century, American social science excelled at steadily improving sample survey data, and public policy has been a beneficiary. So has public understanding of what and who we are as a nation. Alternative information sources will require new attention to data quality and accessibility while still protecting privacy and confidentiality. Social science should again be at the forefront of ensuring that information is a public good.

Notes |

INTRODUCTION

1. Congressional office of Ron Paul, press release, March 28, 2000.
2. Individuals could request a census form in Spanish, Chinese, Tagalog, Vietnamese, or Korean or get help from language assistance guides printed in forty-nine languages.
3. Although we are primarily concerned with census behaviors rather than census knowledge, research has also found a participation gap following from the same logic (see, for example, Berinsky 2005; Eveland and Scheufele 2000). And even the research focused exclusively on knowledge levels typically assumes a fundamental link between knowledge and behavior.
4. There is considerable debate among academics regarding the extent of the decline in civic engagement and social capital documented by Robert Putnam (2000). For criticisms of this thesis, see Ladd (1999), Levi (1996), Skocpol and Fiorina (1999), and Tarrow (1996).
5. The data collection was funded by a consortium of private foundations, including the Russell Sage Foundation, the Ford Foundation, the William and Flora Hewlett Foundation, the Annie E. Casey Foundation, the John D. and Catherine T. MacArthur Foundation, the Andrew W. Mellon Foundation, and the Carnegie Corporation of New York. Norman Nie and Jane Junn were the principal investigators of the survey collection.
6. Knowledge Networks' panel recruitment methodology uses the quality standards established by selected RDD surveys conducted for the federal government. All telephone numbers have an equal probability of selection, and the sampling is done without replacement from the entire U.S. telephone population who fall within the Microsoft Web TV network (87 percent of the U.S. population fall within this network). Selected numbers are called, and the head of household is informed that the household has been selected to join the Knowledge Networks panel. The household cooperation rate during this time averaged 56 percent. Detailed information on the Knowledge Networks

methodology and comparisons of probability versus volunteer Internet samples can be found on their website at: http://www.knowledgenetworks.com/
ganp/index.html and http://www.knowledgenetworks.com/info/press/
papers/Volunteer%20white%20paper%2011-19-03.pdf.

7. We conducted all analyses using weights provided by Knowledge Networks.
Poststratification weights, benchmarking to Current Population Survey (CPS)
distributions on demographic benchmarks for age, gender, ethnicity, region,
and education, reduce the sampling variation. They include a nonresponse
adjustment using the demographic data of those who were initially selected
but who did not complete the surveys.

8. The individual completion rates for each of the monitoring surveys: monitor 1
(83 percent), monitor 2 (82 percent), monitor 3 (61 percent), monitor 4 (58 percent), monitor 5 (64 percent). The differences in completion rates generally
reflect differences in the fielding period.

CHAPTER ONE

1. The text of this chapter was drafted primarily by Kenneth Prewitt and draws
on his experiences as director of the U.S. Census Bureau from 1998 to 2001.

2. We make reference here to two distinct measures of census mail-back cooperation: the mail-back response rate and the mail-back return rate. The
response rate refers simply to the percentage of census forms returned out
of all mailed out by the Census Bureau. Census forms are mailed or delivered using a master address file, and when that file is compiled, the Census
Bureau does not know which houses or apartments are occupied. It is not
until a form has been delivered, not returned, or followed up with a personal
visit that the bureau learns whether a given residency is occupied or vacant.
It takes many months to complete all the checks required to determine the
vacancy rate of households on Census Day, which can be as high as 10 percent of the residencies in the United States. After vacancies and other address
errors are subtracted, the Census Bureau has a list of valid occupied households. Using that as the denominator, it calculates a mail-back *return rate.* In
1990 the return rate was 75 percent, or 10 percent higher than the initially
announced response rate. See figure 1.1 for an apples-to-apples comparison
of response rates, including the 2000 estimated response rate. We discuss the
distinction between the response rate and the return rate in greater detail
later in the chapter.

3. The Census Bureau has used two methods to estimate net undercount figures:
a demographic analysis, and in 2000, a separate post-enumeration survey,
termed the Accuracy and Coverage Evaluation (ACE) survey.

4. Erroneous inclusions might include, for example, a child born after April 1, a
person who died before April 1, or a college student living away from home but

counted in the parents' house instead of at his or her usual place of residence. For brief discussion of duplicates in the census and census error more generally, see Prewitt (2003/2005, 33–37). For a more technically detailed discussion, see Citro, Cork, and Norwood (2004, 240–43, 409–16).

5. A limited list includes Baim (1991), Bradburn (1992), Brehm (1993, 1994), Davis, Mohler, and Smith (1994), Fan (1994), Groves (1989), Groves and Lyberg (1988), Remington (1992), Schorr (1992), Singer and Martin (1994), Steeh (1981), and Yamada and Synodinos (1994).

6. The National Election Study, conducted by the Survey Research Center of the University of Michigan.

7. This CDC survey, known as the Behavioral Risk Factor Surveillance System, is used to plan, initiate, and support health promotion and disease prevention programs, and it monitors progress toward achieving health objectives. The median cooperation rate across the states was 64 percent in 1987 and 47.3 percent in 2001. See http://www.cdc.gov/brfss/technical_infodata/quality.htm.

8. CMOR's 2001 Respondent Cooperation and Industry Image Study, available at http://www.cmor.org/rc/evtpubs.cfm.

9. Notably, turnout in the 2004 election increased to at least 1992 levels, but the trend since the 1950s is still negative.

10. The Jefferson method of using greatest divisors (a fixed ratio with rejected fractional remainders) was the apportionment formula used until 1830. With this method, a ratio of persons to representatives was selected, and then the population of each state was divided by the number of persons. The resulting whole number of the quotient was the number of representatives each state received (fractional remainders were not considered). For a more detailed discussion, see Anderson (2000).

11. Baker v. Carr, 369 U.S. 186 (1962), held that the federal courts have jurisdiction to consider constitutional challenges to redistricting plans. Then, in Wesberry v. Sanders, 376 U.S. 1, 8 (1964), the Court ruled that congressional districts must be drawn so that "as nearly as is practicable one man's vote in a congressional election is . . . worth as much as another's."

12. In 2000, for example, personnel conducting the census and those conducting the independent sample worked out of different offices and reported to different field managers.

13. Matching errors were just one of the problems that led the bureau to not use this system in 1980.

14. The passage cited presents only one of the reasons presented by the secretary; other considerations were technical and operational.

15. Jim Nicholson, memo, May 20, 1997. The Census Bureau itself does not collect information on political party affiliation, does not conduct analysis of possible partisan outcomes, and took no position on the plausibility of Nicholson's forecast.

16. Sampling was to be used in two ways, one of which was in connection with dual system estimation. The initial design also called for sampling as part of nonresponse follow-up, that is, during the phase that employs face-to-face enumeration of households that failed to mail back their census form. This use of sampling was not central to the political controversy that continued into early 2001 and is not described here. For discussion, see Citro et al. (2004).

CHAPTER TWO

1. For discussion of how modifications in census procedures led the Census Bureau to alter its expected mail-back response rates from an initial 55 percent to 61 percent, see Prewitt (2003/2005, 30).
2. Fienberg was so confident that the mail-back rate would not reach 61 percent that, with the chief statistician of the United States as a witness, he made a $100 bet with the recently sworn-in director of the Census Bureau, who at the time naively presumed that the American public would respond positively to the mobilization campaign.
3. There was also the concern that the census forms completed by enumerators would not properly scan if subjected to rain, crumpling, or other damage.
4. The overcount in the 2000 census is reviewed in Prewitt (2003/2005, 36–37) and analyzed in much greater technical detail in Citro et al. (2004).
5. One of the weaknesses of our research design is that the advertising campaign had started before we had the funds to initiate data collection. By the time of our first interview wave, there had already been "census awareness" advertising and rather extensive media coverage. Even the census itself started much earlier than the official Census Day of April 1. For weather and logistical reasons, the census starts in Alaska in mid-January. This staggered beginning presented an opportunity to have a "first person in the census" event that made the front pages of newspapers across the nation—often accompanied by photo 2.1.
6. The Census Bureau director preached more than once before predominantly black and Hispanic church audiences, citing as his Old Testament text the Book of Numbers, chapter 1, and as his New Testament text the second chapter of the Book of Luke. He pointed out that these biblical censuses were extractive (conscription and taxation, respectively), while the American census was designed to send power and funds from the government to the people. The SIQSS census monitor data cannot confirm, unfortunately, whether these sermons improved census cooperation rates.
7. Political advertising exposure measures are also frequently criticized on the argument that recall is correlated with political interest (Price and Zaller 1993). Logically, we would expect such an argument to be inconsequential to our analysis given that attention to census ads is unlikely to be primed by an

exogenous interest in the census or even politics. The census is an extremely low-salience event with a message that is not as complex as, say, a policy debate. We find that the correlation between political interest and our exposure measure is negligible (less than 0.07).

8. Each respondent was shown one or two of the seven ads, on a random basis. In monitors four and five, each respondent saw two videos (out of seven). In monitor two, each respondent saw one video out of four.

9. This initial high level of agreement and stability across the time series was true of blacks and whites, with some slight movement (from 76 to 83 percent) for Hispanics.

10. The Census Monitoring Board was an independent commission established as part of the compromise between the Clinton White House and congressional Republicans during legal and budgetary battles over the census in 1998. Its task, as its name implies, was to monitor the census and report its findings to the president and the Congress. The board's four Republicans and four Democrats seldom agreed about census matters, and therefore they generally wrote separate reports; those by the Republican members worried that the bureau was too invested in its sampling design, and those by the Democratic members offered an antidote to the Republican message.

11. We get similar results using self-reported exposure measures.

12. The knowledge measure is a dummy variable indicating that the individual knows that the census is required by law. We were able to evaluate individual-level changes in census knowledge when the same question was asked again in a follow-up survey in May and June 2000 that resurveyed respondents who had been sampled in one of the monitors.

13. Predicted probabilities are calculated holding all other variables to their means and indicator variables to zero. Substantively, this means that probabilities are calculated for a middle-aged, average-educated, unmarried, white male.

14. We again use the coefficients to predict the probability of mail-back cooperation holding all other variables at their means and indicator variables to zero for various levels of census knowledge.

15. This relationship also holds up to a multivariate test in which census knowledge is regressed on campaign exposure and hearing about the census from others, political interest, political knowledge, education, and other demographics.

16. Predicted probabilities are calculated for each level of advertising recognition holding all other variables at their means and indicator variables at their mode (calculated for those who did not know the census is required by law and did not learn that information during the campaign).

17. The overall cooperation rates among Hispanics are perhaps skewed given that the survey was conducted in English only. As an imperfect check of this discrepancy, we compute differences between respondents who spoke English at home compared to those who did not. As expected, those who did not

speak English at home had lower levels of census knowledge (0.50 versus 0.54) and census cooperation (0.75 versus 0.84), but the non-English-speaking households were slightly more likely to have been exposed to the census campaign.

18. It takes many months to complete all the checks required to determine how many households are vacant on Census Day, which can be as many as 10 percent of the residencies in the United States. After vacancies and other address errors are subtracted, the Census Bureau has a list of valid occupied households. Using the number of valid households as the denominator, it recalculates the mail-back *return rate*. This corrected calculation is a more meaningful indicator of civic responsibility. In 1990 it was 75 percent—or 10 percent higher than the initially announced "response rate." But of course, as Census 2000 got under way, the bureau was again forced to talk about the response rate, because it was the only measure available to compare 1990 and 2000 as the census was being conducted. Long after the census had disappeared from public view, the Census Bureau completed all of its evaluations and determined the final *return* rate for 2000.

19. No doubt similar in this regard to the tendency of the public to report higher voter turnout than, in fact, occurs. Voter validation studies have found that between 7 and 15 percent of respondents indicate that they voted when in fact they did not (Traugott 1989). Voter validation research has concluded, however, that overreporting is not consequential for multivariate results because the individuals who typically feel compelled to lie about voting are not very different from those who do vote. We replicated our model here using data from an NORC survey in which census responses were validated against actual completion, and we similarly find that advertising exposure is related to higher levels of census cooperation. In the NORC replication, advertising exposure was a self-reported measure, and the model could not control for marital status, urban/rural geographic area, and work status. The model controlled for census knowledge but was not longitudinal, so it could not assess the effect of changes in census knowledge.

20. This body of literature usually looks at disparities in socioeconomic status, which is typically measured by education levels, but given differences in education levels by race, the predictions still hold for other related inequalities.

21. This research tends to explain the increasing inequalities that come from information campaigns as attributable to cognitive skills, differences in prior information, discussant effects, and selective exposure to information (Holbrook 2002).

22. Partial because the black-white differential remained high. The black population was undercounted at 1.84 percent and the white population overcounted at 1.13 percent, producing a nearly 3 percent differential—lower than that reported in 1990, but not insignificant either statistically or substantively.

CHAPTER THREE

1. We were, of course, sensitized to privacy issues by what had happened in other countries, especially Germany and the Netherlands. These cases are discussed in chapter 5.
2. One of the authors of this book, Kenneth Prewitt, was director of the census at the time. Although he had been instrumental in helping Knowledge Networks design the initial monitoring surveys, he played no part in the decision to mount the special survey or the experiment specific to the privacy controversy. Nor did he advise on the content or design of these particular studies. Early results from the studies were made public by Knowledge Networks, and he did comment on them in a congressional hearing. Jane Junn, while working with the Stanford Institute for the Quantitative Study of Society, played a major role in the design and analysis of the experimental study. While discussing the results from the experimental study, we are largely drawing from work she conducted as part of the research team.
3. Political psychology research suggests that the source of an elite message influences the effectiveness of the message (Druckman 2001). In other words, the privacy message should resonate most strongly with Republicans and conservatives.
4. The privacy change variable is calculated by subtracting each respondent's question response in the follow-up survey from the respondent's question response in the monitoring survey in which they were included (each respondent was included in one of five monitoring surveys). The results remain unchanged if we restrict the analysis to those respondents who were first interviewed before the privacy debate erupted.
5. Because some personality types may be more susceptible to the issues raised by the privacy debate, we reestimated the model adding an independent variable that measured personal trust. As expected, respondents who indicated that "generally most people can be trusted" were more likely to mail back their census form and the effects of other variables did not change.
6. We held all other variables constant by setting their values to their means (and indicator variables to zero), varying only the values for the change in privacy concern.
7. For Knowledge Networks respondents, who were familiar with short web-based questionnaires, this was an unusually long and tedious survey, with an average completion time of more than thirty minutes.
8. Only questions that should have been validly answered by the respondent were counted as skipped questions. For example, skipped questions on the location and dates of military service were not counted as skipped questions for those respondents who had not served in the military.

9. One possible explanation is that the positive treatment group was burdened by the additional introductory screens. Another possibility is that the control group was not very different from positive treatment because of the pervasiveness of positive census mobilization campaign.

10. Here we have used *return* rates rather than *response* rates. Return rates, which are based on a different denominator, are always higher than response rates. The latter include forms sent to housing units whose vacancy cannot be determined until after a nonresponse leads to that conclusion. After it is able to limit the household universe to inhabited households, the Census Bureau calculates a return rate. The differential rates of cooperation between the short form and long form are nearly equivalent whether the response or the return rate is used.

CHAPTER FOUR

1. The focus of the ads, however, was not so much on "what you can do for your country" as on "what your country can do for you" (Lowenthal and Levine 2000). The message proposed for the 2010 census campaign by Melinda Crowley (2003) makes the assumed relationship between community involvement and census participation even more explicit.

2. Explaining further, Putnam (2000, 348) notes that "it is not surprising that one of the best predictors of cooperation with the decennial census is one's level of civic participation."

3. Edwards and Wilson (2003) suggest instead that the bureau stress the message that participation is required by law, which they show to have had a positive effect on return rates, and messages that grab the attention of younger adults and those who speak languages other than English and Spanish at home.

4. Of course, this does not always happen, leading the Census Bureau to impute the characteristics of the nonrecorded household member (Citro et al. 2004, 126–29). The imputation procedure emphasizes that it is the household, not the individual, that constitutes the basic census unit of data collection.

5. In the multivariate analysis, we create a single measure of the number of organizational memberships.

6. For subsequent analysis, we combine these seven activities into a single additive measure by summing the responses to create an index of civic activities.

7. Sixty-six percent of SIQSS respondents reported voting in the 1996 election.

8. Although it is often assumed that census cooperation and voting behavior are civic activities that are closely linked, we find in fact a rather weak correlation of just 0.21 between reported voting and reported census cooperation— substantially less than would be expected given the emphasized connection in the literature between the two dimensions of civic engagement. Of the nonvoters, 70 percent said they returned their census form. Of the voters, 87 per-

cent claimed to have returned their census form. Bivariate findings, however, are often only reflections of relationships among omitted variables in the model.

9. All other variables are held at their mean or mode for indicator variables. So, the hypothetical respondents are forty-four-year-old, politically independent, working, urban-dwelling, white females with at least some college education.

10. Although not presented here in a figure, the number of years an individual has lived in the same neighborhood also affects the probability of voting, but not census cooperation. For the average person new to a neighborhood, the likelihood of voting is 76 percent; for the same hypothetical person who has lived in the neighborhood more than ten years, the likelihood increases to 81 percent. No such effect is seen on census cooperation. The probability of cooperation is the same for those who have lived in the neighborhood for less than one year or up to ten years, and only slightly higher for those who have lived in the neighborhood more than ten years.

CHAPTER FIVE

1. This chapter was drafted primarily by Kenneth Prewitt and draws on his experiences as director of the Census Bureau from 1998 to 2001.

2. The estimates in this paragraph are based on an anticipated 50 percent initial mail-back response to the ACS survey, an additional 10 percent response to follow-up phone interviews, and then a direct enumeration of one-third of the remaining non-responding addresses.

3. The partisan battle in 2000 was about dual system estimation and adjusting for an undercount/overcount. The current planning for the 2010 census does not anticipate census adjustment. As reported by census director Louis Kincannon, the bureau has concluded that "science is insufficiently advanced to allow making statistical adjustment" in the time frame within which redistricting data have to be released (cited in Prewitt 2003/2005, 37).

4. We note, however, that a 2005 public opinion survey reports that 66 percent of the public favor "requiring all Americans to carry a national ID card" as a means of preventing terrorist attacks. (USA TODAY/CNN/Gallup Poll, July 22–24, as reported in USA TODAY, August 4, 2005, p. 3A.)

5. Because only one-sixth of households received the long form in 2000, this example makes the highly unrealistic assumption that all four residencies would have received the census long form.

6. The census cost $500 million less than the $7 billion appropriated by the Congress for the 2000 census.

References |

Albany (N.Y.) Times Union. 2000. "Census Rules Ensure Privacy, Clinton Says." April 2.

Anderson, Margo J. 1988. *The American Census: A Social History.* New Haven, Conn.: Yale University Press.

————. 2000. *Encyclopedia of the U.S. Census.* Washington, D.C.: CQ Press.

Anderson, Margo J., and Stephen E. Fienberg. 1999. *Who Counts: The Politics of Census-Taking in Contemporary America.* New York: Russell Sage Foundation.

Ansolabehere, Stephen, and Shanto Iyengar. 1995. *Going Negative: How Attack Ads Shrink and Polarize the Electorate.* New York: Free Press.

Atkin, Charles K., and Lawrence Wallack, eds. 1990. *Mass Communication and Public Health: Complexities and Conflicts.* Newbury Park, Calif.: Sage.

Baim, Julian. 1991. "Response Rates: A Multinational Perspective." *Marketing and Research Today* 19(2): 114–19.

Bartels, Larry M. 1993. "Messages Received: The Political Impact of Media Exposure." *American Political Science Review* 87: 267–85.

Bates, Nancy, and Sara K. Buckley. 2000. "Exposure to Paid Advertising and Returning a Census Form." *Journal of Advertising Research* 40(1–2): 65–74.

Bauder, Mark, and D. H. Judson. 2003. "Administrative Records Experiment in 2000 (AREX 2000): Household Level Analysis." *Census 2000 Experiment Report.* Washington: U.S. Census Bureau.

Belden Russonello and Stewart Research and Communications. 1999. "Generating Greater Participation in the 2000 Census Analysis from a National Survey Conducted for U.S. Census Monitoring Board." Available at: http://www.brspoll.com/Reports/Census%20summary.pdf (accessed December 5, 2005).

Berelson, Bernard R., Paul F. Lazarsfeld, and William N. McPhee. 1954. *Voting: A Study of Opinion Formation in a Presidential Campaign.* Chicago: University of Chicago Press.

Berinsky, Adam. 2005. "The Perverse Consequences of Electoral Reform in the United States." *American Politics Research* 33(3): 471–91.

Bowers, Dianne K. 2001. "The U.S. Research Industry and Privacy" (March). Available at: http://www.researchinfo.com/docs/legwatch/2001_03.cfm (accessed December 5, 2005).

Bradburn, Norman M. 1992. "Presidential Address: A Response to the Nonresponse Problem." *Public Opinion Quarterly* 56: 391–98.

Brehm, John. 1993. *The Phantom Respondents: Opinion Surveys and Political Representation.* Ann Arbor: University of Michigan Press.

———. 1994. "Stubbing Our Toes for a Foot in the Door? Prior Contact, Incentives, and Survey Response." *International Journal of Public Opinion Research* 6: 45–63.

Brehm, John, and Wendy Rahn. 1997. "Individual-Level Evidence for the Causes and Consequences of Social Capital." *American Journal of Political Science* 41 (July): 999–1023.

Brewer, Paul R. 2002. "Framing, Value Words, and Citizens' Explanations of Their Issue Opinions." *Political Communication* 19: 303–16.

Bryant, Barbara, and William Dunn. 1995. *Moving Money and Power: The Politics of Census Taking.* New York: New Strategist Publications.

Bulmer, Martin. 1979. *Censuses, Surveys and Privacy.* New York: Holmes & Meier Publishers, Inc.

Butz, W. P., and Scarr, H. A. 1987. "The 1987 German Census: A Trip Report." Report prepared for the U.S. Bureau of Census.

Choldin, Harvey M. 1988. "Government Statistics: The Conflict Between Research and Privacy." *Demography* 25: 145–54.

Citro, Constance F., Daniel L. Cork, and Janet L. Norwood, eds. 2004. *The 2000 Census: Counting Under Adversity: Report of a Panel to Review the 2000 Census.* Washington: National Academies Press/Committee on National Statistics of the National Research Council.

Cohn, D'Vera. 2000. "Census Too Nosy? Don't Answer Invasive Questions, GOP Suggests." *Washington Post,* March 30.

The Columbian (Vancouver, Wash.). 2000. "Puck Hits Bump, Numbers Game." March 18.

Congressional Record. 1987. U.S. Congress, Senate, 9 October 1987, 14011–12.

———. 1988. "Proceedings and Debates of the 100th Congress, Second Session." 134(1): 3-1466. (January 25–February 16). Washington: United States Government Printing Office.

Council for Marketing and Opinion Research (CMOR). 2003. "Respondent Cooperation and Industry Image Study." Available at: http://www.cmor.org/rc/evtpubs.cfm (accessed December 5, 2005).

Couper, Mick P., Eleanor Singer, and Richard A. Kulka. 1998. "Participation in the 1990 Decennial Census: Politics, Privacy, Pressures." *American Politics Quarterly* 26(1): 59–80.

Crowley, Melinda. 2003. "Generation X Speaks Out on Civic Engagement and the Census: An Ethnographic Approach" (June 17). Available at: http://www.

census.gov/pred/www/rpts/Generation%20X%20Final%20Report.pdf (accessed December 5, 2005).

Curran, James. 2002. *Media and Power*. London: Routledge.

Davis, James A., Peter Ph. Mohler, and Tom W. Smith. 1994. "Nationwide General Social Surveys." In *Trends and Perspectives in Empirical Social Research*, edited by Ingwer Borg and Peter Ph. Mohler. Berlin: Walter de Gruyter.

———. 2004. "National General Social Surveys." In *Trends and Perspectives in Empirical Social Research*, edited by Ingwer Borg and Peter Ph. Mohler. Berlin: Walter de Gruyter.

Druckman, James N. 2001. "On the Limits of Framing." *Journal of Politics* 63(4): 1041–66.

———. 2004. "Priming the Vote." *Political Psychology* 25: 577–94.

Edwards, W. Sherman, and Michael J. Wilson. 2003. "Evaluations of the Census 2000 Partnership and Marketing Program." Census 2000 Testing, Experimentation, and Evaluation Program Topic Report 6. Washington: U.S. Census Bureau.

Ebony. 2000. "Why the Census Is Important to You: African Americans' Civil Rights" (April). Available at: www.findarticles.com/p/articles/mi_m1077/is_6_55/ai_61619013 (accessed on December 5, 2005).

Ettema, James S., James W. Brown, and Russell V. Luepker. 1983. "Knowledge Gap Effects in a Health Information Campaign." *Public Opinion Quarterly* 47: 516–27.

Eveland, William P., Jr., and Dietram A. Scheufele. 2000. "Connecting News Media Use with Gaps in Knowledge and Participation." *Political Communication* 17: 215–37.

Fan, David P. 1994. "Predicting Public Opinion from Press Coverage." *The Public Perspective* 5: 21–24.

Fay, Robert E., Nancy Bates, and Jeffrey Moore. 1991. "Lower Mail Response in the 1990 Census: A Preliminary Interpretation." Paper presented to the 1991 Annual Research Conference of the U.S. Census Bureau. Arlington, Va. (March 17–20).

Finkel, Steven E., and John G. Geer. 1998. "A Spot Check: Casting Doubt on the Demobilizing Effect of Attack Advertising." *American Journal of Political Science* 42: 573–95.

Fitzpatrick, John C., ed. 1939. *The Writings of George Washington from the Original Manuscript Sources, 1745–1799*. Vol. 31. Washington: U.S. Government Printing Office.

Fox, Susannah, Lee Rainie, John Horrigan, Amanda Lenhart, Tom Spooner, and Cornelia Carter. 2000. "Trust and Privacy Online: Why Americans Want to Rewrite the Rules." Washington, D.C.: Pew Internet and American Life Project.

Fukuyama, Francis. 1995. *Trust: The Social Virtues and the Creation of Prosperity*. New York: Free Press.

Gantz, Walter, Michael Fitzmaurice, and Euisun Yoo. 1990. "Seat-belt Campaigns and Buckling Up: Do the Media Make a Difference?" *Health Communication* 2: 1–12.

Gaziano, Cecilie, and Emanuel Gaziano. 1996. "Theories and Methods in Knowledge Gap Research Since 1970." In *An Integrated Approach to Communication Theory and Research*, edited by Michael B. Salwen and Don W. Stacks. Mahwah, N.J.: Lawrence Erlbaum.

General Accounting Office (GAO). 2001a. "2000 Census: Review of Partnership Program Highlights, Best Practice for Future Operations." Report to Congressional Requesters, GAO-01-579 (August). Available at: http://www.gao.gov/new.items/d01579.pdf (accessed December 5, 2005).

———. 2001b. "2000 Census: Significant Increase in Cost per Housing Unit Compared to 1990 Census." Report to Congressional Requesters, GAO-02-31.

Groves, Robert M. 1989. *Survey Errors and Survey Costs.* New York: John Wiley and Sons.

Groves, Robert M., and Lars E. Lyberg. 1988. "An Overview of Nonresponse Issues in Telephone Surveys." In *Telephone Survey Methodology*, edited by Robert M. Groves, Paul P. Biemer, Lars E. Lyberg, James T. Massey, William L. Nicholas II, and Joseph Waksberg. New York: John Wiley and Sons.

Hakim, Catherine. 1979. "Census Confidentiality in Britain." In *Censuses, Surveys, and Privacy*, edited by Martin Bulmer. New York: Holmes and Meier.

Heer, David M., ed. 1968. *Social Statistics and the City.* Cambridge, Mass.: Joint Center for Urban Studies.

Hillygus, D. Sunshine, and Simon Jackman. 2003. "Voter Decision Making in Election 2000: Campaign Effects, Partisan Activation, and the Clinton Legacy." *American Journal of Political Science* 47: 583–96.

Hobbs, Frank, and Nicole Stoops. 2002. "Demographic Trends in the Twentieth Century." Census 2000 Special Reports, series CENSR-4. Washington: U.S. Government Printing Office/U.S. Census Bureau.

Holbrook, Thomas. 1996. *Do Campaigns Matter?* Thousand Oaks, Calif.: Sage Publications.

———. 2002. "Presidential Campaigns and the Knowledge Gap." *Political Communication* 19(October): 437–54.

Holmes, Steven A. 2000. "Defying Forecasts, Census Response Ends Declining Trend." *New York Times,* September 20.

Hyman, Herman H., and Paul B. Sheatsley. 1947. "Some Reasons Why Information Campaigns Fail." *Public Opinion Quarterly* 11: 412–23.

Inglehart, Ronald. 1999. "Postmodernization Erodes Respect for Authority, but Increases Support for Democracy." In *Critical Citizens*, edited by Pippa Norris. Oxford: Oxford University Press.

Iyengar, Shanto. 1991. *Is Anyone Responsible? How Television Frames Political Issues.* Chicago: University of Chicago Press.

————. 2001. "The Method Is the Message: The Current Stage of Political Communication." *Political Communication* 18: 225–29.

Junn, Jane. 2001. "The Influence of Negative Political Rhetoric: An Experimental Manipulation of Census 2000 Participation." Paper presented to the annual meeting of the Midwest Political Science Association. Chicago (April 21).

Kenworthy, Tom. 2000. "Some Census Workers Feeling the Heat of Hostility, Suspicion: 'People Feel That Somebody Out There Is Watching.' " *USA Today,* May 2.

Klapper, Joseph T. 1960. *The Effects of Mass Communication.* New York: Free Press.

Krosnick, Jon A., and LinChiat Chang. 2001. "A Comparison of the Random Digit Dialing Telephone Survey Methodology with Internet Survey Methodology as Implemented by Knowledge Networks and Harris Interactive." Unpublished paper, Ohio State University, Columbus.

Kwak, Nojin. 1999. "Revisiting the Knowledge Gap Hypothesis: Education, Motivation, and Media Use." *Communication Research* 26(4): 385–413.

Laan, Paul van der. 2000. "The 2001 Census in Netherlands: Integration of Registers and Surveys." BISNIS project 100049/06. Statistics Netherlands, Division for Social and Spatial Statistics. Available at: http://www.ccsr.ac.uk/conference/vanderlaanpap.doc (accessed December 5, 2005).

Ladd, Everett. 1999. *The Ladd Report.* New York: Free Press.

Lasswell, Harold D. 1927. "The Theory of Political Propaganda." *American Political Science Review* 21(3): 627–31.

Lazarsfeld, Paul F., Bernard R. Berelson, and Hazel Gauzet. 1948. *The People's Choice: How the Voter Makes Up His Mind in a Presidential Campaign.* 2nd ed. New York: Columbia University Press.

Leggieri, Charlene, and Ruth Ann Killion. 2000. "Administrative Records Experiment in U.S. Census 2000." Washington: Planning, Research, and Evaluation Division, U.S. Bureau of Census.

Levi, Margaret. 1996. "Social and Unsocial Capital: A Review Essay of Robert Putnam's *Making Democracy Work.*" *Politics and Society* 24: 45–55.

Lippmann, Walter. 1922. *Public Opinion.* New York: Free Press.

Lowenthal, Terri Ann, and Felice J. Levine. 2000. "Census 2000: Counting on a Civic Moment." *ASA Footnotes* 28(1): 1–3.

Luepker, R. V., D. M. Murray, D. R. Jacobs Jr., M. B. Mittelmark, N. Bracht, R. Carlaw, R. Crow, P. Elmer, J. Finnegan, and A. R. Folsom. 1994. "Community Education for Cardiovascular Disease Prevention: Risk Factor Changes in the Minnesota Heart Health Program." *American Journal of Public Health* 84: 1383–93.

Maccoby, Nathan, and Douglas S. Solomon. 1981. "Heart Disease Prevention: Community Studies." In *Public Communication Campaigns,* edited by Ronald E. Rice and William J. Paisley. Beverly Hills, Calif.: Sage Publications.

Martin, Elizabeth A. 2001. "Privacy Concerns and the Census Long Form: Some Evidence from Census 2000." Paper presented at American Statistical Association,

Proceedings of the Section on Survey Research Methods (August 5–9, 2001). Available at: http://www.amstat.org/Sections/Srms/Proceedings/.

Mayer, Thomas S. 2002. "Privacy and Confidentiality Research and the U.S. Census Bureau Recommendations Based on a Review of the Literature." Research Report Series: Survey Methodology 2002-01. Washington: U.S. Bureau of the Census, Statistical Research Division. Available at: http://www.census.gov/srd/papers/pdf/rsm2002-01.pdf (accessed December 5, 2005).

McCarty, Michael. 2004. "Campaign Hits Broad Target: Everybody Ads Drive Return of Census Forms." *USA Today*, April 24.

Melnick, Daniel. 1981. "The 1980 Census: Recalculating the Federal Equation." *Publius* 11: 39–65.

Mosbacher, Robert A. 1991. "Decision of the Secretary of Commerce on Whether a Statistical Adjustment of the 1990 Census of Population and Housing Should Be Made for Coverage Deficiencies Resulting in an Overcount or Undercount of the Population." *Federal Register* 56(140, July 22): 33583.

Moynihan, Daniel Patrick. 1977. "The Most Important Decision-Making Process." *Policy Review* 1: 89–93.

National Coalition on Black Civic Participation. 1999. Press release, November 1.

National Conference of State Legislatures. Redistricting Task Force. 1999. "Redistricting Law 2000." Available at: http://www.senate.leg.state.mn.us/departments/scr/redist/red2000/red-tc.htm (accessed December 5, 2005).

National Research Council. 2005. "Expanding Access to Research Data: Reconciling Risks and Opportunities." Washington, D.C.: National Academies Press/Panel on Data Access for Research Purposes, Committee on National Statistics.

Nelson, Thomas. 2004. "Policy Goals, Public Rhetoric, and Political Attitudes." *Journal of Politics* 66(2): 581–605.

Nelson, Thomas E., Rosalee A. Clawson, and Zoe Oxley. 1997. "Media Framing of a Civil Liberties Controversy and Its Effect on Tolerance." *American Political Science Review* 91(3): 567–84.

Nie, Norman H., and D. Sunshine Hillygus. 2001. "Education and Democratic Citizenship: Explorations into the Effects of What Happens in Pursuit of the Baccalaureate." In *Education and Civil Society*, edited by Diane Ravitch and Joseph Viteritti. New Haven, Conn.: Yale University Press.

Nie, Norman H., Jane Junn, and Kenneth Stehlik-Berry. 1996. *Education and Democratic Citizenship in America*. Chicago: University of Chicago Press.

O'Connor, Terry. 1991. "Identifying and Classifying Reasons for Nonresponse on the 1990 Farm Costs and Returns Survey, SRB Research Report SRB-91-11." Washington: National Agricultural Statistics Service, U.S. Department of Agriculture.

Perloff, Richard M. 2003. *The Dynamics of Persuasion: Communication and Attitudes in the 21st Century*. Mahwah, N.J.: Lawrence Erlbaum Associates.

President's Commission on Federal Statistics. 1971. *Federal Statistics: Report of the President's Commission*. Vol. 1. Washington: U.S. Government Printing Office.

Prewitt, Kenneth. 2003/2005. "Politics and Science in Census Taking." In *The American People: Census 2000*, edited by Reynolds Farley and John Haaga. New York: Russell Sage Foundation. (Orig. pub. by Russell Sage Foundation and Population Reference Bureau.)

———. 2004. "What If We Give a Census and No One Comes?" *Science* 304(5676, June 4): 1452–53.

Price, Vincent, and John Zaller. 1993. "Who Gets the News? Alternative Measures of News Reception and Their Implications for Research." *Public Opinion Quarterly* 57(2): 133–64.

Putnam, Robert D. 1995. "Bowling Alone: America's Declining Social Capital." *Journal of Democracy* 6(1): 65–78.

———. 2000. *Bowling Alone: The Collapse and Revival of American Community.* New York: Simon & Schuster.

Remington, Todd D. 1992. "Telemarketing and Declining Survey Response Rates." *Journal of Advertising Research* 32: 6–7.

Robertson, Leon S. 1976. "The Great Seat-belt Campaign Flop." *Journal of Communication* 26(4): 41–45.

Rosenstone, Steven J., and John Mark Hansen. 1993. *Mobilization, Participation, and Democracy in America.* New York: Macmillan.

Saluter, Arlene F. 1992. "Marital Status and Living Arrangements: March 1992." Current Population Reports. Population Characteristics, series P20-468. Washington: U.S. Bureau of the Census.

Schorr, Daniel. 1992. "Bad News for Pollsters." *New Leader* 75(May 4): 3.

Shaw, Daron R. 1999. "The Effect of TV Ads and Candidate Appearances on Statewide Presidential Votes, 1988–1996." *American Political Science Review* 93: 345–61.

Sheppard, Jane M. 2001. "2001 Respondent Cooperation and Industry Image Study: Overview and Trends." The Council for Marketing Opinion and Research. (March 6). Available at: http://www.bmra.org.uk/documents/277.ppt (accessed December 5, 2005).

Singer, Eleanor, and Elizabeth Martin. 1994. "Survey Confidentiality." *AAPOR News* 22: 1, 4.

Singer, Eleanor, Nancy Mathiowetz, and Mick Couper. 1993. "The Impact of Privacy and Confidentiality Concerns on Survey Participation." *Public Opinion Quarterly* 57: 465–82.

Singer, Eleanor, Theresa F. Rogers, and M. B. Glassman. 1991. "Public Opinion About AIDS Before and After the 1988 U.S. Government Public Information Campaign." *Public Opinion Quarterly* 55: 161–79.

Singer, Eleanor, John Van Howeyk, and Randall J. Neugebauer. 2003. "Attitudes and Behavior: The Impact on Privacy and Confidentiality Concerns on Participation in the 2000 Census." *Public Opinion Quarterly* 67: 368–84.

Skocpol, Theda, and Morris P. Fiorina. 1999. "Making Sense of the Civic Engagement Debate." In *Civic Engagement in American Democracy*, edited by Theda Skocpol and Morris P. Fiorina. Washington, D.C.: Brookings Institution.

Sniderman, Paul M., and Sean M. Theriault. 2004. "The Structure of Political Argument and the Logic of Issue Framing." In *Studies in Public Opinion: Attitudes, Non-attitudes, Measurement Error, and Change,* edited by Willem E. Saris and Paul M. Sniderman. Princeton, N.J.: Princeton University Press.

Stadt, Huib van de, and J. Mathieu Vliegen. 1992. "An Alternative for the Census? The Case of the Netherlands." Paper presented to the Annual Research Conference. Arlington, Va. (March 22–25). Reprinted in *Proceedings of the 1992 Annual Research Conference.* Washington: U.S. Department of Commerce, Census Bureau, Economics and Statistics Administration (November).

Star, Shirley, and Helen M. Hughes. 1950. "Report of an Educational Campaign: The Cincinnati Plan for the United Nations." *American Journal of Sociology* 55: 389–97.

Steeh, Charlotte G. 1981. "Trends in Nonresponse Rates, 1952–1979." *Public Opinion Quarterly* 45: 40–57.

Survey Sampling, Inc. 2001. "Unlisted Rates of the Top 100 Metropolitan Statistical Areas" (August 23). Fairfield, Conn.: Survey Sampling.

Tarrow, Sidney. 1996. "Making Social Science Work Across Space and Time: A Critical Reflection on Robert Putnam's *Making Democracy Work.*" *American Political Science Review* 90(2): 389–97.

Tichenor, Philip, George Donohue, and Clarence Olien. 1970. "Mass Media Flow and Differential Growth in Knowledge." *Public Opinion Quarterly* 34: 159–70.

Traugott, Santa. 1989. "Validating the Self-reported Vote: 1964–1988." National Election Study Technical Report 34. Ann Arbor: University of Michigan.

Triplett, Timothy. 2002. "What Is Gained from Additional Call Attempts and Refusal Conversion and What Are the Cost Implications?" Working paper, Urban Institute. Available at: http://mywebpages.comcast.net/ttriplett13/tncpap.pdf (accessed December 5, 2005).

U.S. Census Bureau. 2000. "Census 2000 Mail Response Rates." Available at: http://www.census.gov/pred/www/rpts/A.7.a.pdf.

U.S. Census Monitoring Board. 1999. *Census 2000: A National Process Requires Local Focus: Report to Congress.* Suitland, Md.: The Board (February 1).

Verba, Sidney, Kay Lehman Schlozman, and Henry E. Brady. 1995. *Voice and Equality: Civic Voluntarism in American Politics.* Cambridge, Mass.: Harvard University Press.

Vigdor, Jacob L. 2001. "Community Composition and Collective Action: Analyzing Initial Mail Response to the 2000 Census." Working Papers Series SAN01-05. Durham, N.C.: Duke University, Terry Sanford Institute of Public Policy.

Viscusi, W. Kip, Joel Huber, and Jason Bell. 2004. "The Value of Regional Water Quality Improvements." Harvard John M. Olin Discussion Paper Series 477

(June). Available at: http://www.law.harvard.edu/programs/olin_center (accessed December 5, 2005).

Vliegen, J. M., and H. van de Stadt. 1988. "Is a Census Still Necessary? Experiences and Alternatives." *Netherlands Official Statistics* 3(3): 27–34.

Walker, Kent. 2000. "Where Everybody Knows Your Name: A Pragmatic Look at the Costs of Privacy and the Benefits of Information Exchange." *The Stanford Technology Law Review* (October): 2. Available at: http://stlr.stanford.edu/STLR/Articles/00_STLR_2/index.htm (accessed December 5, 2005).

Wallack, Lawrence. 1990. "Two Approaches to Health Promotion in the Mass Media." *World Health Forum* 11(2): 143–64.

Weakliem, David, and Wayne Villemez. 2004. "Public Attitudes Toward the Census: Influences and Trends." *Source Social Science Quarterly* 85(4): 857–71.

Westin, Alan. 2000. "Intrusions: Privacy Tradeoffs in a Free Society." *Public Perspectives* (November/December): 10.

Wolfinger, Raymond E., and Steven J. Rosenstone. 1980. *Who Votes?* New Haven, Conn.: Yale University Press.

Wolter, Kirk, Bob Calder, Ed Malthouse, Sally Murphy, Steven Pedlow, and Javier Porras. 2002. "Partnership and Marketing Program Evaluation: Census 2000 Evaluation." Chicago: National Opinion Research Center.

Word, David L. 1997. "Who Responds/Who Doesn't? Analyzing Variation in Mail Response Rates During the 1990 Census." Working paper 19. Washington: U.S. Census Bureau, Population Division.

Yamada, Shigeru, and Nicolaos E. Synodinos. 1994. "Public Opinion Surveys in Japan." *International Journal of Public Opinion Research* 6: 118–38.

Yanovitzky, Itzhak, and Courtney Bennett. 1999. "Media Attention, Institutional Response, and Health Behavior Change: The Case of Drunk Driving, 1978–1996." *Communication Research* 26(4): 429–53.

Yanovitzky, Itzhak, and Jo Stryker. 2001. "Mass Media, Social Norms, and Health Promotion." *Communications Research* 28: 208–39.

Zaller, John R. 1992. *The Nature and Origins of Mass Opinion.* New York: Cambridge University Press.

Zanutto, Elaine, and Alan Zaslavsky. 2002. "Using Administrative Records to Improve Small Area Estimation: An Example from the U.S. Decennial Census." *Journal of Official Statistics* 18(4): 559–76.

Index |